EXECUTIVE
LONELINESS

The 5 Pathways to Overcoming Isolation, Stress, Anxiety & Depression in the Modern Business World

by

NICK JONSSON

EXECUTIVE LONELINESS

The 5 Pathways to Overcoming Isolation, Stress, Anxiety & Depression in the Modern Business World

#1 INTERNATIONAL BESTSELLER

1st Edition 2021
ASIN: B091B1Y3WZ (Amazon Kindle)
ISBN: 979-8-71867-536-8 (Amazon Print)
ISBN: 978-1-64633-587-9 (Ingram Spark) PAPERBACK
ISBN: 978-1-64633-588-6 (Ingram Spark) HARDCOVER
ISBN: 978-1-00591-392-2 (Smashwords)

Contact the Author: Nick Jonsson
Business Name: EGN Singapore
Author Website: https://nickjonsson.com
Main Website: https://executivelonelinessbook.com
LinkedIn: https://nickjonsson.com/linkedin
Book Bonus: https://executiveloneliness.community/bonus
Email: nij@egn.com & nick.jonsson@gmail.com
Phone: +65 8618 3872

Source: Successful But Lonely at the Top, The Business Times, 28 February, 2020 (SPH-ID: 33351877) *The Business Times* © Singapore Press Holdings Limited. Reprinted with permission in the publication.

Source: Lonely Leaders, *The Sunday Times*, 31 May, 2020 (SPH-ID: 34617647) *The Straits Times* © Singapore Press Holdings Limited. Reprinted with permission in the publication.

Font type: Myraid Pro

Font size: content - 11pt/Chapter title - 22pt

Table of Contents

Book Bonus:
Join Our Free Community

It doesn't have to be lonely at the top. Join our community and get access to our ever-growing tips and resources. In addition, you can access the links mentioned in this book.

Your journey is yet to begin until you start to implement the ideas in this book. After all, implementation and action-taking are the real keys to success.

Visit
https://executivelonelinessbook.com/page/bonus
to join our community and get access
Executive Loneliness Resource Kit

Scan the QR Code Below

Dedication

This book is written in memory of my working colleague and friend, Simon Greaves, who died of suicide in 2019.

It is also dedicated to my wonderful family—the Jonsson's—my mother, father, and sister, with her family and friends—who have supported me through my recovery journey. There are too many lovable people to mention one by one. You know who you are. I need, however, to give one special mention, and that is to my lovely wife, Dona Amelia, who was by my side 24/7 for months during my darkest hours and never gave up on me, even when I had almost given up on myself.

This book is also dedicated to my ex-wife, and my son, who had to suffer by my side when I was sick. I am sure that many things I said or did back then, made little sense to you. I apologize for the damage my illness and selfish behavior caused you.

Love to all my colleagues, friends, partners, advisory board members, speakers, chairs, and members at EGN who supported me continuously through my recovery journey. You have donated both time and money to the charity campaign "Race to an End of Executive Loneliness", and have helped me with surveys, interviews, and agreed to share experiences for this book.

Also, I am grateful to the support group for problem drinkers that I joined in May 2018; a group that clearly saved my life. I will forever be grateful to my old Bond University friend in Singapore who put me in contact with the group, and to my good friend who was there for me in the first meeting, and remains there for me today. I am forever grateful for the meetings and our bike rides.

A final remark and blessings to the Samaritans of Singapore (SOS), and the beautiful suicide prevention hotline in Singapore, for the wonderful work that you do. I am blessed to have done a charity project with you, and I will continue to give you my love and support.

About the Author

Nick Jonsson is dedicated to raising awareness and eliminating the stigma around the phenomenon of executive loneliness. He has identified that feelings of isolation and depression—personal struggles that he, himself, has had to grapple with and conquer—are much more widespread than we think.

Modern work culture encourages executives to project success and achievement when, in fact, thousands actually suffer in silence and denial. This topic is close to Nick's heart. He has spoken about it multiple times, on the radio and television, at conferences, exhibitions, company events, and chambers of commerce, and he has been featured in more than 20 newspaper and magazines articles, including a four-page feature in The Business Times and a full-page in The Straits Times.

As the co-founder and managing director of the Singapore branch of EGN (Executives' Global Network), Nick is passionate about matching senior executives in confidential peer groups where they can help each other face challenges and identify opportunities.

Having worked across Asia, Australia, and Europe representing major international firms, Nick has acquired expertise in international general management, direct sales, and marketing. He has also been entrusted to serve as the vice-chairman of the Nordic Chamber of Commerce in Ho Chi Minh City, and the vice-chairman of the AmCham Vietnam Direct Selling Committee, positions that further demonstrate his ability to add value on a global scale. He is highly self-motivated and enjoys participating in marathons and Ironman events. Nick also thrives on the adrenaline of speaking at conferences, seminars, and events.

Nick is enthusiastic about supporting his local community. He is a volunteer and fundraiser for the Samaritans of Singapore (SOS), a suicide hotline in Singapore. He also does frequent community service for a support group for problem drinkers. Now in recovery himself in his third year, he is also an International Coaching Federation (ICF) coach, who loves to work with executives to help them with their career and lifestyle choices.

Nick holds a bachelor of communication degree (marketing and advertising) and a master's in public relations from Bond University, Australia, where he graduated top of his class.

You can read more information about Nick on his LinkedIn page:

https://nickjonsson.com/linkedin

You can also see Nick's website here:

www.nickjonsson.com

What People Say About Nick Jonsson

Nick recently made an inspiring virtual presentation on Executive Loneliness to Mentoring Men in Australia (@mentoringmen). Our group of 100+ matches volunteer male mentors to other men who are seeking someone to talk with and confide in about the life challenges they are facing. Nick guided us through his own personal story and shared how accepting our own vulnerability and being able to open up to others can produce a powerful and life-changing effect on our future. Of all the keynote speakers to address Mentoring Men, Nick has been the most relevant and engaging, and we look forward to working with him again in this vital area to support mental health in the workplace.

—John Ogier, Director of Learning & Enablement at Total Inter Action

Nick conducted a webinar for our company where he shared on the topic of overcoming the stigma of mental illness. During this challenging period, we launched a mental wellness campaign for our employees where we wanted everyone to not neglect their mental health. I am very glad that Nick was part of this campaign where he shared useful tips and resources. He also shared his personal experiences which made it very personable and real. Thank you again, Nick!

—Amanda Lui, Learning and Development Executive at Heinemann Asia Pacific

Nick is passionate about mental health among executives. He is sincere and authentic in all his interactions. He was a keynote speaker for our "Hear More 2020" event, and our customers were inspired by his journey and resilience. Nick's workshop/talk illuminated the nuances of executive loneliness that many feel but don't talk about. If you are looking to inspire your team or customers - especially during these difficult times, I would highly recommend Nick.

—Sharad Govil, Managing Director at GN Group

Authentic leadership isn't a phrase I use often, but when I think of Nick, this phrase immediately comes to mind. Nick has shown time and time again his ability to authentically connect with people through compassion and empathy. He believes in genuine relationships and is a true "network connector", who is very well respected and admired amongst his peers. Nick's dedication to raising awareness by openly discussing mental health and executive loneliness has helped break down the barriers of this important topic. I have had the privilege of listening to his keynote and was immediately drawn in by his passion, vulnerability, and thought leadership.

—Michael Henry, Chief Technology Officer at Singapore Sports Hub

Nick has a great story of resilience and the courage to tell it. His message on overcoming executive loneliness is an important one for everyone to hear because the consequences are deadly serious. Nick walks his talk and shows that it is not weak, but strong, to ask for help. I was honored when Nick asked me to coach him to craft his message and delivery so that he could fulfil his mission to bring awareness and action. I highly recommend Nick as a speaker to anyone who wants to add life-saving value to their conference.

—Andrew Bryant, Founder at Self Leadership

Nick put on a really good show on behalf of EGN last night. He gave a super emotional talk on his personal journey in dealing with executive stress, loneliness, depression, and related problems. Very thought-provoking. There was a really engaged audience representing the great-and-the-good of downtown Singapore, and it was nice to rub shoulders with some old friends too. Looking forward to the next event, Nick.

—Alexander Mearns, Founder at Levitise—Lifestyle, Nutrition, and Fitness Centre

Nick was one of my speakers speaking at PrimeTime Professional & Business Women Association. During the many occasions we were working together, Nick is always humble, dedicated, and committed to the cause. He inspires me and with his authenticity and resilience.

—Ling Chong, Regional Lead, Talent Management & Learning Development (APAC) at Panalpina

Nick is a brave and inspiring professional who brings taboo topics to light. We need more successful people like Nick, who embrace and share about depression and suicide. Being fearful to speak about it won't make these issues disappear. Discussing them openly, on the other hand, brings awareness and a sense of belonging. Continue with the great work, Nick!

—Sandra Quelle, Chief Happiness Officer & Career Coach at The Happy Mondays Co.

Nick Jonsson is a person who has drive, ambition, and a willingness to perform. Nick works with his heart and inspires others to commit to targets by simply being himself. Nick sees the big picture as well as adapts to changes around him. Nick's creativity and rapid approach make him a leader that leaves no stone unturned. He delivers and does so together with his team.

—Frederic Sebastian Widell, VP & Head of SEA & Managing Director India at Oriflame Cosmetics

We simply could not have marked World Suicide Prevention Day on 10 September better. For that, we have to thank our guest speaker Nick Jonsson, managing director of EGN Singapore. Nick gave one of the most authentic, courageous, and open presentations we have ever hosted. His topic was executive loneliness, which, if not recognized and treated, can result in substance abuse, wrecked lives, lost jobs and relationships, and, at its very extreme, suicide. As we all know, society still stigmatizes mental illness, which very often prevents people from seeking the help they need. Men especially. Thankfully, Nick did seek help. His best friend did not and died by suicide.

—Victor Mills, Chief Executive, Singapore International Chamber of Commerce

You can find more than 50 recommendations of Nick on this page:

https://nickjonsson.com/linkedin

Foreword

By Andy Lopata, author of Connected Leadership and Just Ask: Why Seeking Support Is Your Greatest Strength

Over the years working and catching up with Nick Jonsson in London, Vietnam, and Singapore, there was never a clue that behind his sunny demeanor, bear hugs, and big, cheesy smile, lay the turbulence he shares in this book.

I have one very vivid image of a conference in Ho Chi Minh City for which Nick booked me to speak. Nick took to the stage as the conference host in a bright pink suit (and when I say bright, I mean—really bright!) and had the audience on their feet, cheering, chanting, and clapping their hands. This was a man in full control, in his element, and at the height of his powers.

At least, that was the impression. And it's often the case that the impression we get, when we see high achievers doing what they do best, can mislead us. We see superhumans, naturally confident, impervious to poor fortune, and on a different level to mere mortals.

And yet, behind the mask, the truth is often very different. For my own book on the topic, I interviewed Hattie Webb who, with her sister, was backing singer to two legendary rock stars, Tom Petty and Leonard Cohen. Hattie shared with me stories of both artists backstage before big concerts, laying bare their stage fright. Leonard Cohen's hand was shaking while pouring a coffee, Tom Petty said that he didn't know whether he could go through with it. Nobody in either audience would have had the tiniest thought that the stars on stage in front of them were petrified at the thought of performing that night.

In this book, Nick shares his own story alongside stories of a number of executives who lay bare their self-doubt, anxiety, work, and family issues, and more. In almost all cases, these crises of confidence are hidden from their charges, all of whom rely on them for leadership and direction.

We have been conditioned over many years to appear strong and to know all of the answers. This is particularly true of senior executives, who are used to being set on a pedestal in their organizations and industries, and who constantly feel the pressure to live up to that billing.

As Nick discusses in the book, we see vulnerability as a weakness and focus on doing what we can to portray strength. I believe that this is exceptionally costly–both to the business and to the individual concerned.

We have a responsibility as individuals, as leaders, and as a society to change this perspective. We need to make it okay to be unsure, to be under pressure, and even to fail. We need to encourage sharing and honesty, for not only is it better for people's mental health, but it also leads to earlier intervention when things do go wrong, to better collaboration, and to more innovation.

I had no idea how Nick was struggling the last few times we caught up with each other. I wish I had known and could have been more help to him. The takeaway: you're not as alone as you sometimes think. Most of us have people who love us and care for us and who want to see us succeed. Those people would be delighted to help us achieve our goals and devastated if they find out that we didn't let them.

Let's see vulnerability as a strength. This book is an important step in that journey and contains stories that resonate and great practical advice that will help. Read to the end, apply the lessons, and then gift a copy of the book to a colleague who may also benefit.

Remember that you are not alone and let others help you. And always remember not to jump to judgements about someone else's life, based on the brightness of their suit or the broadness of their smile.

Introduction: What Is Executive Loneliness?

Senior executives under immense pressure to excel have few avenues to vent their fears and frustrations. In turn, this can cause them to feel isolated. This feeling of isolation, in combination with their feelings of stress, fear, and frustration, can lead to depression, anxiety, insomnia, and other similar dysfunctions. This is executive loneliness. And because the executive is in a high-profile position, they can get stuck in this dysfunctional lonely state, and it can end up being detrimental. Detrimental to their health, their relationships at home and at work, and to their whole outlook on life.

Part of being an executive is leading companies to success; as such, when an executive is experiencing executive loneliness, they often do nothing to address it for fear of appearing unsuccessful. Of course, not addressing it exacerbates it, and the negative, difficult feelings continue and increase.

That's what this book is about—exposing executive loneliness and bringing to the forefront an honest discussion about:

- The pressures of being an executive,
- The fact that executive loneliness is actually quite common, though typically hidden, and
- The five primary ways an executive can emerge stronger and better from this difficult place.

Dr Glenn Graves is a psychologist and life coach who works closely with senior executives who have gotten trapped in executive loneliness. This is how he described executive loneliness as it exists in many of his clients: "What I tend to see are executives feeling growing anxiety or lethargy. They may become impatient and withdraw from normal social interactions. They often experience an overwhelming doubt, pessimism, or loneliness. This state of mind can lead to the potential for impulsivity or less-than-healthy forms of coping and escapism. Alcohol or other forms of substance abuse, or shallow and more transactional relationships are what I see most often in my practice. If they don't find support, this could eventually lead to suicidal ideation and even suicide."

As you'll read in the chapters about my own story, I have firsthand experience with executive loneliness as a very real and life-threatening condition, which motivated me to author this book. However, my story is for a later chapter.

Presently, let's turn to a former executive, who we are referring to as "George."

George's Experience of Executive Loneliness

As companies work through the COVID-19 outbreak, George worries about the mental health impact—what I'm calling "executive loneliness"— that it might have on C-suite executives. George lives in Singapore and knows the financial stress a crisis like this puts on businesses. When Lehman Brothers collapsed in 2008, his food and beverage company lost 50 percent of its revenue for nine months, forcing him to sell his entire business.

For George, it was heartbreaking, to say the least, to spend 14 years building something only to lose it all. At the height of its success, his company earned a prestigious World Gourmet Summit award. George himself received a nomination for Ernst & Young Entrepreneur of the Year. He sat on the boards of various organizations, and people regularly sought his advice on expansion into China.

But by 2009, his dream life started to unravel. A month after he lost his company, his wife filed for divorce. He fell ill and stayed home alone to recuperate. Left to his own devices with few friends to confide in, he sank into depression and thought of suicide, both of which are detrimental but not uncommon aspects of executive loneliness. Here's how George relayed his story to me:

I had gotten so used to being chauffeured around and wearing bespoke clothes. Everyone was nice to me because they wanted to get great service when they went to my restaurants. I shook hands with ministers. Aspiring entrepreneurs knew my name.

But when I lost my company, people started avoiding me. The phone stopped ringing, and the only people knocking on my door were debt collectors. When your business fails, people don't remember the ten good things you did before that–like supporting young entrepreneurs or helping the country's F&B industry develop–they just remember that your business failed. You go into a tailspin, and suicidal thoughts emerge. I fantasized many times about jumping off my building because I was so depressed. But, luckily, there were moments of grace that saved me.

I remember a friend who came by and we didn't talk the whole night—we just watched soccer. I don't even like soccer, but I stared at the TV screen for 45 minutes because I was just happy to be sitting next to my friend, who cared enough to just spend time with me. There's no judgment—that was important.

Another time, a friend asked me out for a birthday lunch. When I arrived, there were a dozen of my friends there. They didn't get me a present, but they each put in US $100 in an envelope and gave me $1,500 or so. It's not the money, of course, that mattered. It's the gesture that moved me.

Eventually, I met a single mother with two kids. Kids, if you don't already know, are great. They don't judge you at all. I played with them when I was there. And I slowly realized there were so many things in life besides career success. And I began to pick myself up and rebuild my life. I'm in my early 50s now and starting a new business. It'll take me some years to grow this one. But, as they say, baby steps.

When you're down and out, you're too depressed to save yourself. The only thing that can save you is human connection. I hope people reading remember that when someone is depressed, it's up to them to reach out and show compassion to the person. They don't have to say anything smart or insightful. Just visit the person and be present—that's enough. That might save that person's life.[1]

Failure is such a taboo topic in the business world that society tends to fail to address it adequately. George noted, "In recent years, the government has started to talk about how Singaporeans should see failure as part and parcel of entrepreneurship, and remove the stigma attached to it. But back in 2009, there was no such recognition … I struggled for years to get back on my feet."

Hans's Experience of Executive Loneliness

Hans, a pseudonym, is a German expatriate who worked for three years as the business development manager for an oil-and-gas service company in Singapore. It was a fairly new company, and he poured all of his savings into it. Hans thought they could sell it later for a lot of money, which would

---

1. *Source: https://www.businesstimes.com.sg/lifestyle/feature/successful-but-lonely-at-the-top*

act as the nest egg for him and his family whom he'd brought with him to Singapore. Here's how Hans explains what happened:

When the oil and gas market collapsed in 2015, the interested party who wanted to buy our company backed out, our Chinese partner backed out, and we were facing US $3 million in debt, with no revenue coming in. We could not fix the problems because it was an industry-wide downturn. It was mayhem.

For much of 2016, I was still going into the office, but I didn't have anything to do. I was anxious and distracted all the time. Even when there were potential opportunities or silver linings, the fear of failure overwhelmed me. I kept thinking I had failed my wife and children. My boss had properties and some inheritance money, so he couldn't really understand what I was going through. We would hang out after work and drink. But that became a spiral that got progressively darker.

Hans's overwhelming feelings and fear of failure are standout characteristics of executive loneliness. Drinking—in particular, drinking too much—is also a common but ineffective way executives try to cope with the loneliness. Hans went on to say this:

Fortunately, I have a good wife who was observing everything that was going on. It was she who pulled me out of it–as things were going south very quickly. When I felt guilty about bringing the family here, she said this was their choice as much as it was mine. She never made me feel bad about myself.

When the company was bought over by a rival, I made many attempts to get another job elsewhere, but they came to naught. I have only an employment pass, and companies didn't want the hassle of the handling of my paperwork. Again my wife came to the rescue, helping me make the decision to start my own events consultancy firm. Even though she had not worked a day since we got married, she started working every day with this startup.

Meanwhile, the friends I thought I had stopped talking to me. They were friendly as long as I had a job and money. But the moment I lost those things, they ceased to care. I imagine that if I was a single expatriate man going through this alone, I might have done something drastic to myself.

My advice to any single ex-pat is to just pack up and go home to the people you love because they're the only ones who can help you through this. If you don't, you may end up looking for sympathy or escape in all the wrong places, and it'll only get you into more trouble. Without the right support system when things go south, you will be in for a very rough ride.[2]

---

2. Source: https://www.businesstimes.com.sg/lifestyle/feature/successful-but-lonely-at-the-top

The "right support system" Hans is referring to is exactly what I aim to supply to you in this book, but more on that shortly. Let's continue to look into executive loneliness and the mental health epidemic.

Leaders Hide Struggles

"While stress is an inevitable component of work-life, the pressure can be particularly acute for men and women at the top," explained Maria Micha, a clinical mental health counselor and corporate trainer with over two decades of practice. "I would say that 100 percent of C-level managers suffer from anxiety. And 70 to 80 percent of them have mild, moderate, or severe depression. About 10 percent have suicidal thoughts–though only a small percentage of that number actually act on it," she says.

Ms Micha also pointed out, "The biggest problem is the taboo surrounding these issues. C-suite execs risk losing their position if they admit they're experiencing depression or contemplating suicide because there's so much riding on the public perception that their companies are doing well … As a result, many of them don't look for help because they're afraid about word getting out."

These are issues this book addresses in order to bring a voice to this typically silent and terrible experience. This book also gives practical tools to executives themselves, so they can support themselves to get out of, and stay out of, the despairing and desperate trap of executive loneliness.

Data Is Scarce

Experts say there is scarce data on how many senior executives suffer from loneliness, depression, or anxiety. A general study by the Institute of Mental Health published in 2018 showed that one in seven people in Singapore, experience a mental health condition in their lifetime. When EGN Singapore, a business networking platform for leaders, conducted a small-sample survey in 2019 among its members, it found that 30 percent of senior executives either currently are in, or have undergone, bouts of depression–higher than the national average cited above–while over 80 percent of them are reluctant to discuss the state of their mental health with their companies.

This reminds us of beloved public figures who seemed to have suffered in silence about their mental health and who died of suicide. There's fashion designer Kate Spade, celebrity chef Anthony Bourdain, comedian Robin Williams, and coffee chain tycoon VG Siddhartha, as well as billionaire Tony Hsieh, the founder of Zappos, who also wrote the book *Delivering*

Happiness. Their cases show us that money, power, and public veneration are not buffers against depression.

Ms Micha notes: "Singapore decriminalized suicide in 2019–which was the right thing to do. For years, I would get calls from potential clients who would ask: 'If I tell you I have suicidal thoughts, would you report me?' Even when I would answer, 'No, never', they were still afraid … If Singapore wants to maintain its position as a business hub, it must also lead the way in corporate mental health." Breaking down this stigma, bringing to light the experience of depression, and assisting executives and their loved ones are issues we address head-on in this book.

Mental Health for All

Many health experts point out that in addition to the mental health issues that executives experience, in reality, it is people working at all levels of a company that are contending with these issues.

Priyanka Bajpai, regional head, Southeast Asia, of the healthcare communications firm SPAG, says: "Mental health is not bound by hierarchy, and anyone is susceptible to issues such as loneliness, anxiety, and depression. The pressure to create a brand for oneself and one's company, to engage in social media and stay publicly visible, to fulfil KPIs and other measures of success, all bear down upon the individual."

"Hence, it's not so much a function of leadership, but the expectation of the individual from themselves, as well as how they manage and perform, while still maintaining sanity in pressure situations. In fact, one could argue that millennials face a greater pressure to project a certain image of corporate success on social media, whereas older executives are more secure of their track record and have their coping strategies in place. The pressures we face are inevitably part and parcel of our contemporary lifestyles today, but the degree to which we prioritize our mental health is the degree to which we can improve and work upon it."

Both Ms Bajpai and Ms Micha note that more organizations are recognizing the importance of mental health and reaching out to experts. The National Council of Social Service in Singapore has a Mental Health Toolkit for employers, that provides resources for employers to support employee mental health. Many companies are teaching employees to reach out to a colleague empathetically when they spot warning signs, such as alcoholism, excessive weight gain, and despondency.

But mental health programs looking specifically at C-suite leaders' struggles, are less common because senior executives prefer to conceal their struggles from staff and shareholders. As Ms Micha put it, "Companies really need to look deeper at the issue if they want to improve their KPIs and increase their sales. Any financial investment in staff counselling will pay back in spades. When an executive is free from the hormones of stress, that's when they can be creative and innovate, seek solutions that were not visible before, and take the company to a higher level. Companies must remove the stigma of anxiety, depression, and mental illness, so employees feel safe speaking about their problems."

Today's Mental Health Epidemic

It is of course not only senior executives that suffer from depression and mental illness. Everyone from all backgrounds is suffering. Executive loneliness is only a part of a much greater mental health epidemic going on in the world today, one that seems to only been rising. Let's look at some evidence that supports this:

- According to studies by Asia Care Group, 91 percent of Singaporeans report feeling stressed, which is seven percent above the global average, and 80 percent report they have an "always-on" work culture, which is 16 percent higher than the global average. This significantly elevated the level of stress costs in Singapore to $3.1 billion annually.

- In 2018, the UK government announced its first suicide prevention minister (BBC). The creation of this post is indicative of how prevalent suicide and mental health issues are in the UK.

- The biggest cause of death in Australian males between 15 and 44 years old is suicide. Similar to executives caught in executive loneliness, a majority of this age group don't talk about their problems.

- Because they recognise how important mental health is, the NYPD and Starbucks have put in the effort and money to provide mental health benefits for their workers. After all, as per the biggest happiness study ever, loneliness is very dangerous for our health.

- Worldwide, for the past 20 years, depression has been cited as the single biggest cause of disability for people.

This Book: Overturning Executive Loneliness, Overturning the Stigma and Opening the Door

While depression certainly affects everyone, from young to old, perhaps it is even more prevalent amongst successful business leaders and entrepreneurs. This is because they might be even more vulnerable to it because of the stresses of their jobs and the traits that brought them success in the first place.

An executive's experience of loneliness, depression, and anxiety is made worse because most don't like to admit that it's happening. They don't seek help or even want to discuss it with those closest to them. Most leaders believe that they can manage on their own, and they slip into overdrive. The very last thing they want to do is to display any weaknesses or vulnerability to colleagues, bosses, owners, or investors. They are paid to be the boss, and they are supposed to be strong. However, success is like an iceberg.

On top, you only see 10 percent, and below is the 90 percent hidden, which includes all the failures, the dedication, the hard work, the loneliness, and the issues. Especially with social media, we only show what we want others to see.

As someone who was once an executive, myself, and who was once trapped in serious executive loneliness for several years, but who managed to emerge, I've made it my mission to draw attention to this typically hidden issue, in order to help as many others who are suffering in silence as I can. That's why I wrote this book.

Herein, I describe my experience of executive loneliness, and you'll read of the struggles of other executives as well. Through these stories, you might recognise aspects of your own struggle that you might not have realised were in fact quite serious. You'll also see that you aren't alone. As important as these stories are, you'll also read of my and other executives' experiences engaging the five-step solution to get out of, and stay out of, executive loneliness. Through this book, expect to be seen, heard, and offered an open door that you can walk through to leave behind that troublesome, debilitating trap forever.

Also, be aware that with this book, we aren't simply trying to overcome executive loneliness and mental health issues. We're also combatting the stigma around mental health, which is the epidemic that we've neglected to talk about. When the stigma is broken and we have an open dialogue about mental health, including executive loneliness, then isolated and silently struggling individuals will find the freedom to be honest and vulnerable, and speak openly about their issues. Executives make up a special subset of these people—outwardly successful, devoted to work, very active in work circles but also isolated, never engaging in the necessary deep and honest conversations with others to feel seen, heard, and to learn to process their struggles. So, that's another big aim of this book: to bring executive loneliness to the discussion table to overturn the stigma.

Nick's Story—Stumbling Into Meltdown

Today, I am full of life, but I have also been to the dark side—caught in the trap of extreme executive loneliness. I share the story of my meltdown and emergence back into the light so that other people—and executives, founders, and business owners in particular—can either avoid or else emerge from the pit of executive loneliness that seems to be very near us, though rarely does anyone talk about it.

Here is my story.

Vietnam

Let me take you back to 2008, when I was living as an expatriate and working as a sales manager for a Swedish company in Vietnam's Ho Chi Minh City. I thought I was doing well, but one day, I was called into the office of my boss, and I was let go. I was furious. This was the first big blow to my international career, and I refused to accept it. Previously, I was a scholarship student at university and graduated at the top of my class. I'd done well in my previous work roles. In fact, I was selected for this particular job in Vietnam out of more than 2,000 candidates when I'd applied. They had hired me with a clear career path as a future managing director of the company. Seeing as I had laid out my success path, I was very disturbed and unhappy about the dismissal.

At home that night, I told my then-wife what happened.

Afterwards, she said: "Nick, we need to talk … " Bam! Just like out of a movie, she announced that she was pregnant. We were going to have a baby.

My world collapsed around me. As you may already know, being a Swedish ex-pat in Vietnam means that everything you have is linked to your job. The house you live in, your visa, your work permit, medical insurance, car, etc... I hadn't lived in Sweden for more than a decade, and at that time I was not very close to my family, so my connections to Sweden were very loose at best. When I lost my job, everything I felt that connected me to my life in Vietnam was suddenly gone, and we had a baby on the way—a child we very much wanted—but I worried about how to provide for the baby.

It felt like the carpet was being ripped out from under me. My whole world collapsed. Work was really all I had. I hadn't imagined that something like this could ever happen to me, and I was woefully unprepared. There was no plan B (something we discuss in a later chapter in this book). My resume and LinkedIn profile were well out-of-date, but most importantly, I was about to become a father and I no longer had a job, house, let alone health insurance, for my then-wife and our new baby.

A lot of questions had to be answered.

- *Were we going to have the baby in Vietnam?*
- *Should we move our lives back to Sweden?*
- *What on earth were we going to do?*

Eventually, we made the decision to stay in Vietnam, and I was able to secure a couple of short-term positions before being offered a more permanent job as general director with a French fashion company, where I began to do well again.

Indonesia

Our son was born in Vietnam in February 2009, and things were beginning to look much better for us. After a few years in my new job, I was given a promotion and asked to move to Indonesia. I relocated with my family to Jakarta. We moved into a new house, and my son, who was then 5 years old, was enrolled in a new school. Two months later, just as he was settling in, I was told that the company was being sold and that, once again, I would be out of a job.

It had already been tough on us as a family to relocate to a new country where we had no friends. Now, to be without a job in a foreign country, not knowing anyone...it sent me into a panic. I had been given a redundancy package, but as any of you who have lost a job will know, it is never enough. The school fees were only paid up until the end of the semester, the house was gone, and our insurance would soon run out. It felt like all the earlier issues from when I was let go in Vietnam had come back to haunt me.

I didn't know what to do. So I did what I think many men who end up in a similar situation do—I put on a brave face for my family. I asked my then-wife to move back to Sweden and to take our son with her. I would remain in Jakarta to try and sort everything out. At least if they were back in the West, there were my then-wife's parents and my parents who could help out, and my boy would have a school to go to. I would know that they were okay.

So, there I was, all alone in a foreign country, in a new city where I didn't really know anybody—both socially or professionally. Once again, I had to settle for short-term job assignments wherever I could find them.

Fortunately, a large medical company I'd done some work for in the past was looking for a deputy general manager to run operations in Indonesia. I applied and was given the job. It was a great position that came with a big package. But as the saying goes: once bitten, twice shy. Although I was constantly being told that I was doing well, I felt terribly scared and anxious. I began to turn to exercise more, and consume more alcohol outside of working hours to relax. I either went to the pub to drink too many beers after work, or got up in the early morning for a run or a bike ride. It seemed like I needed some kind of escape to cope with life, and this would later become a big problem.

I felt suspicious of my colleagues and would anxiously open my inbox at the start of every day, expecting a message from my boss calling me into her office to be dismissed. Whenever I did receive a message that she wanted to meet with me, I was sure that she was going to tell me that I'd been let go. The level of insecurity I was feeling because of past events built up to such an extent that after about a year and a half in the position, I walked into my boss's office and resigned. I resigned for no other reason than I could not face being fired for a third time. I wanted to get out first, just in case they were privately contemplating letting me go.

This is obviously quite a strange thing to do, but I genuinely thought that if I took control, if I took the initiative, if I resigned before being let go, then it would all be done and dusted. I really didn't know what I was doing and I definitely didn't have a solid plan B. But at that time, this move made sense to me.

When I announced my resignation to the bosses, they were completely shocked. They asked, "What's wrong? Don't you like Indonesia? Do you want to move to Dubai instead? Do you want to move to the US? We have many roles for you. You're doing so well. Why do you want to leave?"

By this time, I had already gone through all the different scenarios multiple times in my head, and I knew I just couldn't be in the job anymore. I'd made up my mind to go. There was no way I was going to reverse my decision. They tried to encourage me to stay. They offered me other opportunities, such as the mentioned options to relocate to Dubai or the US, but I declined them. My decision to leave left me feeling lonely and lost inside. As I had no close friends, I made this decision on my own without talking to anybody about it. Though I didn't know it, I was, and had been for a while, caught in a deep pit of executive loneliness and mental turmoil. The loneliness meant I was feeling homesick, but was I missing Sweden, where I was born and grew up, or was it Vietnam, where I'd lived for so many years? Perhaps I'd be happy if I moved back to Ho Chi Minh City?

Vietnam, Again

At this point, I was too scared to move back to my home country Sweden. Since going back there would mean that I had to, as an adult, return home without a job and stay with my parents. This would not look like success but a failure, something which I was not interested in. So, I left Indonesia abruptly and asked a friend to sell all my belongings at a garage sale as I moved by myself back to Vietnam. Although I felt more at home in Vietnam, I was without a permanent job, alone without my then-wife and our son, and without a future.

I found myself jumping from part-time job to part-time job and becoming more and more unhappy. Eventually, EGN, Executives' Global Network, called me up. They wanted someone to help them set up a few peer groups in Ho Chi Minh City. I accepted the offer and the project. I built up a team and three peer groups with 75 members in Ho Chi Minh City. After I completed the project, the company was then acquired by a local player in Vietnam. This happened just as a managing director position at EGN opened up in Singapore.

I was in a bad state in Vietnam. The hole of executive loneliness I found myself in was only getting deeper. I was falling into the trap of drinking too much, not sleeping enough, and generally not looking after myself. Singapore, as a more modern country and a more "European" country, seemed like a better compromise. I had the idea that there might be more support for me there. Maybe I could make some close friends, and maybe I could get professional support, including the medical attention that I, by this stage, needed.

Singapore

With a desire to start making some important lifestyle changes, I grabbed the opportunity and moved to Singapore in January 2018. And there I was in yet another new city—unhappy, isolated, lonely, and unwell. The new job meant starting all over again, including getting a new visa, new work permit, new bank account, new home, and new furniture. At least I'd made the move.

As there hadn't really been anyone on the ground recently, looking after the company I was taking over, I found myself having to work hard to get the business up and running. As many of you will understand, when business is tough, we tend to spend much of our energy focusing on the tasks at hand while neglecting the well-being of those around us, including ourselves. It will not be a surprise, then, to learn that I found myself working around the clock, shoring up EGN's cashflow, and going to the pub for too many drinks after work in order to relax.

Although heading out to the pub after work helped me relax and forget about work for a while, I was waking up feeling awful, and the hangovers quickly grew worse. I had to take valium and benzodiazepine in the mornings to calm my nerves or I would not be able to cope. I was trapped in a vicious downward spiral, and after just a few months, I had gained nearly 20 kilograms in weight. I was deteriorating both physically and mentally, and I seriously thought I might be having a breakdown. This was executive loneliness on overdrive.

Most people around me seemed to have no idea what was going on. I am pretty good at putting up a front, but behind the façade, something this book addresses in the chapter Smiling Depression, I felt like I was dying. With nobody to speak to about my problem, I made the decision to seek professional help. However, I was paranoid about seeing a doctor in Singapore, in case somebody recognized me in the surgery, so I went to see doctors in Indonesia and Thailand instead. It is important to admit to readers that I, at this stage, was so ill that I was dependent on either alcohol and/or valium or lorazepam, to cope with just living a normal day. There was no way I could go 24 hours without these substances.

I tried to stop cold turkey on a few occasions, but the withdrawal symptoms from the alcohol and drugs would give me terrible delirium tremens (DTs) that left me shaking, shivering, sweating, and with an irregular heart rate. I would even develop a fever. I later on learnt that alcohol is one of the most dangerous drugs from which to withdraw. Fortunately, most people will never go through this terrible experience since delirium tremens

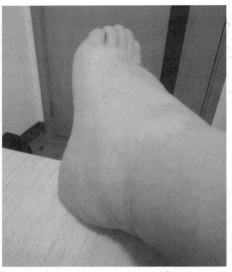

typically only occurs in people with a high intake of alcohol for more than a month,[1] and I had been drinking for more than one year at this stage. I can clearly remember these days as the most painful and scariest of my life.

The Final Straw

Unfortunately, just as everything seemed to be looking up, my left foot swelled up. Later, this condition was diagnosed by Maria Micha, a clinical mental health counselor, psychotherapist, and hypnotherapist, as a psychosomatic symptom of the major depressive disorder I had been living with for years. The chronic anxiety and depressive symptoms that were untreated, resulted in a manifestation in my body via the swelling. When emotional and mental pain is not released or processed, our bodies will experience disease. Whether this was to do with the anxiety or the medicine I was taking to treat my executive loneliness, my foot was so swollen that I couldn't even put on socks or shoes.

This was the final straw.

Seeing a specialist doctor in a psychological ward in Thailand, I was finally getting the emergency medical help and medicine I needed to be able to stop the alcohol. This was on May 5, 2018, and I have, at the time of writing this book, not had any alcohol since. It was not an easy transition. I was on strong medication and felt drowsy and experienced a loss of coordination, headaches, nausea, blurred vision, etc., but at least I could go one day, then two days, and more, without consuming alcohol. I started to grasp at a slim hope of life coming back. I started to believe that I might just survive this. However, although I was feeling a bit better, I was not happy.

My recovery was further helped by the fact I'd met someone I felt I could share my problems with. I had met a woman who was about to become my new wife, Dona Amelia.

I was convinced that my life was over, meaning I was convinced that I was in the process of dying, and, as such, I was experiencing extreme

1. *Source: https://en.wikipedia.org/wiki/Delirium_tremens*

anxiety and panic attacks. I genuinely thought I might die, especially as the doctors had no idea what was wrong with me. I was not, however, suicidal. It was then that I started to prepare for the worst and get my affairs in order. I signed up for life insurance and wrote my will. I sent the documents to my parents and my ex-wife in Sweden with instructions. I genuinely wanted everything to be in place in case my health suddenly gave up on me.

I also decided to do some research into my family and discovered that, on my father's side, the average age of death for males was 44. At the time of writing this, I am now 45. Back then, I was 42, and my anxiety was exacerbated by the knowledge that I might have only a couple of years left to live. Although this increased my stress levels, there was a certain amount of relief in knowing that there was no way I could combat genetics. I was powerless to fight against the inevitable.

Thankfully, by this point, I was married to my new wife, and I was starting to share things with her honestly and openly. She was the first person I honestly and openly talked to. I started to recover, slowly, one step at a time. I will talk more about my recovery in the next chapter.

Real Tragedy

Then, real tragedy struck. A good friend of mine, Simon, died by suicide. He was due to speak at one of my company events. He had worked in the recruitment sector for a few years and had some great ideas about the "future of work", which he would present in an event we were hosting. We'd met a few times over coffee to prepare for the event, and he seemed genuinely excited about giving his presentation.

I'd invited Simon to attend another event we were putting on, so he could get a better idea of what to expect on the day. Although he said he would be there, he failed to turn up. At the time, I thought no more about it because no-shows are not uncommon at events like these in Singapore.

The following morning, I received a message informing me that Simon had passed. I was in complete shock, as was everyone who knew Simon. He had never shown any sign that things were difficult for him. We all assumed he was living the dream. He had just come back from fulfilling his ambition of making it to base camp at Everest. He had a girlfriend he was very much in love with. His Facebook page was packed with happy photos and comments. On the outside, everything looked perfect, thus another tragic example of "smiling depression", which just goes to show we may never really have any idea what is going on beneath the surface.

Simon's death due to suicide was a huge eye-opener for me. I'd never talked to anyone about my own very dark times, and after I started my recovery, I'd only ever talked about the difficult stuff with my wife, Dona Amelia, and members of the support group that I'd joined.

Simon's suicide changed all this. I now felt compelled to speak up. I knew I needed to help. I knew I needed to share my story. I knew I needed to help other executives to share their stories. I now felt I had the courage to help other executives who might be having similar feelings. I knew there must be people out there who had been suffering and who were suffering still. I needed to share the message. But first I needed to get in contact with Simon's family. I connected with Simon's brother in the UK and asked permission to talk publicly about what had happened and whether I could use Simon's name. I was relieved when he said, "Absolutely, Nick. Feel free to shout it out loud. Simon wouldn't mind, and I certainly don't."

Shouting It Out Loud

That's what I decided to do: shout it out loud. And so, a few weeks after Simon's death, I launched a campaign called "Race to an End of Executive Loneliness." I posted a LinkedIn announcement about the launch of the campaign, explaining that all money raised would be donated to the Samaritans of Singapore (SOS), an organization dedicated to providing confidential emotional support to individuals facing a crisis, thinking about suicide, or affected by suicide. The post quickly went viral, and people from around the world started writing to me. I received many, many heartfelt, anxious messages, for example:

- *Nick, my wife has had suicidal thoughts from time to time, and I have struggled to find someone to talk to openly about this. Thank you so much for raising awareness of this issue which makes it easier to talk about.*

- *Nick, I attempted suicide myself last year and am now recovering. Thank you for talking about a subject most don't touch. It gives me hope when more people understand this issue.*

In the next chapter, I'll summarize my recovery journey through the five steps.

Book Bonus:
Join Our Free Community

It doesn't have to be lonely at the top. Join our community and get access to our ever-growing tips and resources. In addition, you can access the links mentioned in this book.

Your journey is yet to begin until you start to implement the ideas in this book. After all, implementation and action-taking are the real keys to success.

Visit
https://executivelonelinessbook.com/page/bonus
to join our community and get access
Executive Loneliness Resource Kit

Scan the QR Code Below

Nick's Story—Steps to Recovery

How do we overcome executive loneliness?

The answer to this question is the biggest goal of this book. Based on my own recovery experience, consultations with mental health experts, conversations with other executives who managed to recover from executive loneliness, and relevant research findings and the literature, as I see it, there are five steps for either recovering from or totally avoiding executive loneliness. This book itself details each of these five steps:

1. Taking Stock

2. Asking for Help

3. Getting Healthy

4. Nurturing Healthy Relationships

5. Finding Your Purpose

In this chapter, I'll summarize my recovery journey through the five steps. Additionally, you can expect me to discuss my own experience with each of these five steps in more detail in the chapters dedicated to the steps. For now, it's just an overview, so you'll know what to expect.

Steps 1 & 2—Taking Stock and Asking for Help

When I reached my lowest point and thought I was literally dying—this was in Singapore in 2018, when I chose to write my will and put my affairs in order—I turned to my new wife, Dona Amelia. It helped me tremendously to have someone I trusted to talk to and confide in. Our talks offered me a genuine turning point and was the start on my road to recovery. Speaking to just one person helped me to open up and face the truth.

Of course, opening up to someone I could trust was only the beginning. For my problems to be resolved, I needed to act. I needed medical attention, and I needed to tell the doctors the whole truth in order to receive proper medical treatment. I also recognized that I was drinking too much, and for this to get better, I needed to be honest with myself. And from there, I needed to be vulnerable and express the whole truth of what was going on with me to the doctors and eventually to others. This is all part of taking stock.

Step 3—Getting Healthy

I knew that taking a week off the booze or trying to quit outright on my own was not going to work. In fact, I'd already tried and could do it for select periods of time, but overall it hadn't worked. I could take time off drinking before, but at this stage I had lost that control. I couldn't do it, and I was getting worse; alcoholism is a progressive disease. So I decided I should start going to a support group for problem drinkers. However, the stigma attached to admitting I had an alcohol problem meant it took me some time to pluck up the courage to actually go to a meeting.

In the end, I contacted someone to take me along to the first meeting, which was a great help. He is still one of my best friends today, and I am forever grateful for his support. That meeting was a key stepping stone in saving my life, and to emerging from executive loneliness.

It worked. At least at the time of writing, it has worked, and if I take it one day at a time, I'm confident that it will continue to work. I haven't had a drink since May 5, 2018. I realized that drinking could not be a part of my life if I was truly going to get better. I replaced drinking alcohol with healthier activities involving exercise, diet changes, changes in my sleeping schedule, and more.

Going to a support group for problem drinkers introduced me to others who were facing the same problems as I was—many of whom were also executives. I learnt that many of them were based in Singapore but spent a great deal of time away from home, traveling all over Asia. This meant spending time alone in hotel rooms, going out for boozy team-building dinners, and spending time in bars. For many busy executives, relaxation goes hand-in-hand with drinking.

Joining a support group for problem drinkers, many of whom were executives like me, meant I could now share my problems with people who understood what I was going through. Suddenly, it was not only my wife whom I could speak to about the challenges I was facing. At last, I was able to be vulnerable and honest, and address my issues, step-by-step, with others. Slowly, I was starting to come back to life.

Step 4—Nurturing Healthy Relationships

I felt hopeful because there were people in the support group telling me that they had been in my situation a year earlier and had managed to overcome their problems. It is rare that, as adults, we are granted the opportunity to have open and honest conversations. In my case, it was with strangers. But when you are open, honest, and willing to share what is going on with you, you get great results (by the way, these are all important issues we address in the chapters about taking stock). The honest conversations I was having at my support group for problem drinkers were also the inspiration behind the Executives' Global Network (EGN) for which I am the co-founder and managing director at the Singapore branch. The organization has been set up to facilitate confidential group discussions for senior executives.

The EGN meetings allow executives to open up about work-related challenges in an honest, safe environment where everyone has signed an non-disclosure agreement to ensure confidentiality. Too often we keep our problems to ourselves instead of opening up and being honest about them. In my case, when I look back, keeping things to myself felt terrible. The decisions I was making were really bad—moving from country to country, resigning when I was doing a great job, getting divorced because I was frightened—I mean, come on, what was I doing?

If I'd had people around me whom I knew and trusted, I would have been able to open up about my problems, and perhaps they could have helped me or stopped me from making some of these bad decisions. Why didn't I talk to my boss about how I felt, rather than making the decision on my own to resign? I didn't give people the chance to help because, at the time, I felt I had to make these decisions alone. So, apart from opening up, connecting with people, being honest, and quitting alcohol, what else did I do to overcome my problems?

As I said, I replaced my lousy coping mechanisms with some healthier activities. I hired a coach, someone who not only trained me to vastly improve my fitness, but also guided me in terms of all aspects of my health, including my overall fitness, sleep, and diet, as well as weight, rest, heart rate, etc. My coach helped me to install apps on my devices to help me further track and manage my eating, my sleep, and my exercise.

As far as exercising goes, to start with, I was so unfit that I began by just walking, and then my program was gradually increased. Seeing my progress and my achievements on a daily basis motivated me to continue to make progress. The pubs and wine bars were replaced with vegetables and a healthier diet. I was beginning to feel much better after just one month of quitting the booze and improving my diet. I was also starting to sleep better. I now monitor the hours and minutes I sleep every night. If I fall behind, I make sure I go to bed earlier the next night, something I still make a top priority.

Step 5—Finding Your Purpose

Another important part of my recovery is making it a point to help others. By speaking up about depression, anxiety, Simon's death by suicide, and my own personal story, I am encouraging others who may be suffering to also come forward and to ask for help. I know that this is working because, after each of my keynote speeches or published articles on the topic of executive loneliness, I am contacted by people who want to thank me or who are seeking help. I am then able to listen to them and give them advice. Admittedly, I am not a medical professional, so I cannot give medical advice, but I can listen and help steer them in the right direction, linking them to experts. If I cannot help, then I know the people to link them to who can. We must always know that we are not alone, and we should never be too shy to ask for help.

And finally, just 14 months after I began my recovery, I completed an Ironman triathlon in Sweden (an Ironman triathlon is a 3.8-kilometer swim, a 180-kilometer bike ride, and a 42-kilometer run). Competing and completing this Ironman was a goal I'd set a year earlier and had worked toward over the year. Forming this goal and working towards it greatly helped me attain focus on my recovery journey. I continue to compete in races, and I believe it shows how we, as humans, are capable of turning just about anything around, no matter how dark things may appear. I've even found that the human body itself yearns to heal and recover, and when we give it a chance by getting healthy, it recovers quickly.

In Simon's honor, I completed the race in 12 hours and 59 minutes to raise awareness and money for Samaritans of Singapore (SOS). As with this book, my aim is to raise awareness about depression, loneliness, and suicide, and to raise awareness about the stigma associated with mental health and suicide in particular. I'm doing this in the hope that things can become better for others. I am extremely proud of my own emergence from executive loneliness and my achievements along the way, and will continue to support the cause.

Recovery and Emergence

Since those dark days in 2018 when I thought that my life was over, my life has improved miraculously in all areas, and I have made more progress in the last two-and-a-half years, than in the 25 years before. I have had my share of problems and disappointments because this is part of life, but I have also experienced a great deal of peace and happiness that comes with inner freedom. I have some close friends now whom I am completely transparent and honest with. I feel connected to these people, and we help each other to overcome hurdles and support each other like I never thought was possible. My friendships these days are built on mutual trust, understanding, and love, without strings and without obligations.

I now live in two worlds. One is the transparent world in my support group where we are honest and open, and the other world is the one where people are putting on a show. I will not put on a show in either world, so I may stand out, because being honest and vulnerable is rare. It is so rare that I even get radio and TV interviews, keynote talks, and media articles written about me. This is how hard, rare, and special it is, to be honest.

Today I am grateful that I have lost both the obsession and urge to drink alcohol. That is not to say that I will never relapse. Life is a rollercoaster, and we must enjoy the ride. However, I have learnt through my recovery journey that we should focus on progress rather than perfection, one day at a time.

I've written this book to give you the tools and also the hope that you too can avoid or recover from the extreme anguish of executive loneliness. In the rest of this section, we'll look more at the nuances of this despairing condition. After that, we will focus on the ins and outs of the five steps to recovery. You'll be hearing from a lot of executives and experts along the way who give advice, share their experiences, and offer their solutions.

No One Talks About It

Because of the stigma around mental health issues and executive loneliness, people suffering from it, for the most part, don't talk about it. Not with their spouses, their good friends, their doctors, and certainly not with those whom they spend the most time with: the people at work. And when you don't talk about it, you get more and more entrenched in it. The stress and negative coping behaviors pile up, which then exacerbates the depression, anxiety, and loneliness. Not talking about it increases your sense of isolation and worsens the anguish. As I've already stated, one of my aims with this book and my whole involvement in campaigning around mental health, is to get people to start talking about it. To combat and erase the stigma. To better people's lives and even to save lives.

Ritu Mehrish, author and executive coach, in explaining the reason why senior executives are so very hesitant about discussing their loneliness, said the following: "As I have mentioned in my book Leader's Block, leaders do feel isolated and lonely at the top. There are not too many people with whom they can share their anxieties, fears, or challenges. These are successful people who are used to being on top of their game. To the world, these leaders are the epitome of success with fancy designations and fulfilling lives. The senior executives don't want to break that notion, so even when they are feeling frustrated or stressed, they don't share that openly. The inner conflict, dilemma, and noise translates into them becoming irritable, short-tempered, moody, volatile, or even withdrawn. It affects their performance, decision-making, and ability to focus, such that before long, they start to doubt their abilities and lose their confidence. When they internalize the frustrations, it starts to spill on their personal front too. The moods are carried home and impact their families. If not corrected, more often than not, it can lead to burnout."

As you read previously, even in my own experience of mental breakdown and executive loneliness, I too was not talking about it. For me to talk about it with my second wife was a major stepping stone. Next, for me to be honest about it with my doctors was huge. After that, for me to not just listen but also tell my own story of struggle in my support group for problem drinkers was a feat. The reason I'm pointing this out is to raise your awareness around the fact that serious internal struggle is likely happening to many people in our lives, but since people don't talk about it, others just don't know, but that doesn't mean they won't sympathize and do all they can to help.

Simon, my friend and colleague, was struggling with the very thing I was struggling with, yet neither of us talked about it. While I too was worried that I would die because I'd gotten so sick, I never wanted to die. Simon actually died by suicide, taking his very life. If only we'd dared to talk, connect, and make steps for recovering together. Supporting one another. Simon's untimely death, along with all those "if only ..." thoughts, moved me to go public.

The tragic ending of Simon's life compelled me to embark on a mission to open up about my own mental health issues. What did I do? I started posting on social media, planning for this book, and doing surveys of colleagues at my office. In 2019, I polled EGN Singapore members and other senior executives in the community on the subject of executive loneliness. Out of a total of 56 anonymous respondents interviewed, 30 percent said that they had suffered from work-related depression. Let's do the math on that: 30 percent of 56 people is about 19 people acknowledging they have suffered from work-related depression. As to whether they found it easy to talk about the subject, 82 percent answered, "Not easy" and "No". Again, this goes back to the subject of this chapter: No One Talks About It. And that obviously contributes to and increases the feelings of stress, isolation, depression, and loneliness. Not talking about it compounds those feelings.

In December 2020, we again surveyed senior executives, asking them the same questions that we asked those senior executives we polled the year before. (To be clear: the executives we questioned in 2020 were part of the same network, but different individuals than those of 2019.) Let's compare those findings. In 2019, 30 percent of the anonymous executives in Singapore had been suffering from depression. In December 2020, this number had doubled to 59 percent. This signifies how the current pandemic has resulted in double the amount of depression cases, among executives who suffer from managing big jobs. Thus, it shows how very real and urgent the message of this book is.

In 2019, 82 percent of the anonymous Singapore executives we talked to, found it difficult to talk about executive loneliness in their company. In 2020, 84 percent said they found it difficult. Sadly, but not surprisingly, it seems that while the people suffering from executive loneliness has doubled since the pandemic, people are still not talking about it in their companies. We have seen only a few people step forward in the public eye to discuss it, while overall, it is a topic that is still not spoken of. Thus, again, the message of this book proves itself even more timely and imperative. Please read this book and see it as vital and important, to you or to someone you care about in your life, for executive loneliness is an ever-growing tragic reality for many people.

When I asked "Alexander"—not his real name—an executive in Singapore, to give his thoughts on how people in leadership positions handle their executive loneliness, here's what he said: "As a leader, I don't even think you can talk about difficulties, challenges, conundrums, being at a loss, and not seeing a way forward. It may depend on the environment you are in, but being a leader, you are expected to be able to deal with those things, and most times you can. But in some cases, you can't, and if there is not a collaborative environment to openly find the core issues, then this is what leads to loneliness. As as you can't address the core issues, then it follows that you are in an environment where you can't talk about loneliness. As an executive, to some extent, you have to accept that it's 'lonely at the top' and find your own way to deal with it."

To reiterate: in this book, I supply multiple tools and practices to help you and other executives "deal with it."

"Maureen"—not her real name—who is also an executive, had a similar experience. She explained it like this: "I experienced executive loneliness first when I first joined a leadership team as the only Asian female director. I was excited, proud, yet concerned about fitting in. But the total ecosystem around me in the leadership scope was very foreign to me and very different from my leadership style. I found decisions were made based on personal relationships and trust, rather than sound business rational. I found off-line conversations overshadowing group consensus, thus making it difficult to establish clarity around team adhesion. So naturally I started feeling lonely and out of place among others. I didn't know how to break the walls and stop being an outsider. I was also concerned to approach the matter in a way that I didn't alienate anyone."

American expatriate in Singapore, David Litteken, is someone who wrestled with this sense of isolation, too. David is senior vice-president in Singapore of a global agency focused on workforce recognition programs and sales loyalty events, employing more than 1,800 staff worldwide. David, who has been living in Singapore for three years, is responsible for business across the Asia-Pacific, including offices in Shanghai, Singapore, Melbourne, and Sydney. This responsibility carries with it a lot of demands, which obviously can be stressful.

When David was working in Shanghai for five years, he remembers feeling alone in a city of 25 million people. He said: "I did not know a single person. None of my leaders and none of my staff. I left an environment where I was well-grounded and had to figure it out for myself."

Rather than allowing the loneliness to build and putting all of his time and effort solely into work, David got proactive. He joined a few chambers of commerce and a dining club for executives. In this way, he started to build a network of expatriates as well as local Chinese friends. As he stated, "That gave me the confidence to reach out further." David's decision to reach out to others and nurture both personal and professional relationships is something we'll look at more in *Step 4—Nurturing Healthy Relationships*.

Radu Talks About It

It took him a year to compose the post, but one day, Radu Palamariu, a top talent scout in supply chain, technology, and transport, wrote a post on LinkedIn where he explained his longtime struggle with depression. He went public and talked about it. Here's how he explained it:

I shared a bit of my story and my challenges that I have experienced over the years, like depression and mood swings that I had been diagnosed with. I made the decision to share it on LinkedIn because I felt that it would be a good idea to encourage people to seek help. I got the idea and I had been thinking about it for a while. I think it took me a year actually [to write the post and publish it]. I think everybody has issues, but it's not very common for people to seek help. And it's not very common for people to share in a more public space. So, my intent was to share that and encourage people to seek help. I think that's first and foremost, because many of the people that struggle with depression struggle in silence, in solitude; they don't even tell their families. So I thought, let's make it public. And hopefully some professionals or ultimately anybody who's posting on LinkedIn, if they resonated with it, then maybe if they have an issue, then they can seek help or get some sort of inspiration or options.

After I posted it, I did not expect such a massive response from people. There were lots and lots of replies. There were some people that shared their own stories, and one person said that, even when just posting a comment, he had to look at it 10 times before he posted it, because it's not something that we're used to in our society—to admit that you are weak, depressed, or not perfect; or that you don't live a perfect life. So I think there were a couple of examples of that, where people also shared their own journeys and struggles. And in general, I think there were over 100 comments. Most agreed that mental health is an issue that needs to be put out in the open and discussed, talked about. It's something that is important. It's something that we need to be talking about more in the workplace. This post and the responses showed the walls we have built up around us. We don't speak about it much. It's definitely a challenge that a number of people face, or somebody they know faces this challenge. Hopefully, we'll talk about it more in the future.

I think we need more people to just recognize we are human. We are not perfect. All of us have our own struggles and we should seek help when we need it. And the help that works for one person might not work for someone else. It's individual. But the point is to seek help.

I also want to say that unlike me, you don't need to blast it out and tell everybody in your company that you're struggling. For example, you could seek help from psychiatrists, therapists, and psychologists. You might have close friends or family you can confide in, or there are other specialists out there. There are so many resources out there. Of course, you could go to your boss and say, "Look, I really need a break from [whatever]." I've done this before with my bosses. And I didn't tell them that I was depressed. I simply told them I really needed a break because I was crashing. A lot of bosses will understand that.

The main takeaway: when you are in a mental health crisis, do not try to fix it yourself. Do not think you are weak. No person is an island. Seek help. Talk about it.

Whole New Life: When You Open Up

The problem when we don't talk about our issues is that we hold them as secrets. In turn, it can happen that we go to great lengths to protect these secrets to make sure no one finds out about them. We do this because we don't want to expose what we perceive as faults or weaknesses to others. In the support group for problem drinkers I attend, I learnt that it is okay to speak up, it is okay to tell the truth, even about the most intimate parts of your life. I learnt that "we are only as sick as our secrets". Therefore, keeping and holding on to our secrets keeps us beholden to our sickness, whether that sickness be anxiety, depression, extreme loneliness, feelings of isolation, or a drinking problem. The way to recovery and freedom is through speaking up.

I have learnt that to maintain my recovery and keep executive loneliness at bay, I must always be transparent and honest. I've learnt to speak about anything that is on my mind and troubling me. In the beginning, it feels a bit awkward, but you get used to it after a while. As a first step, I started by sharing with my wife only. Then after a while, I began talking with the fellows in the support group. As I started to see the benefits of speaking up, I also started to tell some more people what was truly going on with me, including family, close friends, and coaches.

It was amazing to experience a whole new world and life opening up to me as I spoke my "secret." I learnt that people will judge you anyway and that is okay, just go on and be your very best, be honest and sincere. Always keep your side of the street clean and you don't have to worry about anything, even if the whole world knows about your secrets, which I guess is now the case with me, since I am revealing all my "secrets" in this very book. The point is that removing yourself from the isolation, anxiety, depression, and stress of executive loneliness is only possible when you are completely transparent. It will take some practice, but get started right away and share your secrets with someone you trust. If you don't have a friend that you can share with, then see a counselor or coach. If your issues are work-related, you can share them in a confidential peer group if you belong to a network such as EGN, where you can discuss and get feedback on your challenges before they turn into problems.

If you do not disclose what is bothering you, past traumas or hurts, or current resentments, you will be less likely to get better because you'll be holding on to those things and keeping them close, even though it's likely not your intention. Take a leap of faith, and share your secrets with your partner, a friend, a counselor, or a coach today. The response will overwhelm you and will be life-changing, for the better.

It's Lonely at the Top

During a radio interview, when I was asked how it feels to be a senior executive, I answered, "It's lonely at the top." Even if you are surrounded by people, you can still feel lonely. I was the managing director of EGN Singapore at the time and I was surrounded by people, but I still felt disconnected because of how I felt inside. Sadly, that's the way executive loneliness works: loneliness even when surrounded by others.

Today, when I'm around people, I feel a connection. Once I put in the effort to enact the five steps for recovery, which we'll be visiting in detail later in the book, something inside me changed. And as long as I continue to put in that effort, I'm confident I will continue to feel connection.

In this chapter, we'll spend some time looking more into that disconnection; that "lonely at the top" feeling. Perhaps you will recognize it in yourself, in someone you know and care about, or even in one of your bosses or colleagues. Recognizing the loneliness is key in order to act to change it and embrace a happy, satisfying life.

Here is how Maria Micha, clinical mental health counselor, psychotherapist, and hypnotherapist, explains why it is so common for top executives to experience serious loneliness:

Being celebrated as good leaders and executives is to exceed those goals. They feel very lonely in their efforts. They don't believe that their team members can understand them. And it's also not their job to understand them. Their wives or husbands, their children, and/or their families also expect them to achieve. They have been achieving all this time. And whatever struggles they're experiencing, they're physically exhausted. They're mentally exhausted, emotionally burned out. They don't have time for themselves. Plus, they simply cannot share their struggle with anyone because if they share it, if they voice it, then it becomes real. They cannot face disappointment in other people's eyes. Whether those others are team members, other team leaders, superiors, spouses, family members, and/or children. All the issues simply make them feel alone, depressed, anxious, obsessive, and suicidal. But they feel that no one would understand and that no one wants to know. So they keep trying until they no longer can. They either have a nervous breakdown or, unfortunately, become suicidal.

From my own experiences and from Maria Micha's observations, it should be evident that executive loneliness is an incredibly serious condition and one that we should put in every effort to understand and help extricate the person from, whether that be a loved one or our own self.

Lonely at the Top

In Singapore, where I live and work, many of the senior executives are regional directors. Therefore, most often they report to offices in Europe, the US, and beyond. They have a team that reports to them from the various countries that they visit once a month or once a quarter. The role of the regional director is to connect with the team to inspire them to achieve their targets. They tend to take their team members out for morale-boosting dinners. But do they really know what's going on with their team members? Do they know whether they are having difficulties? Are you ever asked by your manager how you are doing without simply giving the answer, "Everything is just fine"? When people who spend so much time together in the work setting never really connect on a deeper level—it sets the stage for disconnection and loneliness to set in, for the director and possibly for the team members too.

And then there is the executive's family. Most often, they stay behind in Singapore when the leader is travelling around the region for business. As a result, the leader is further disconnected from the one group of people you would think they would be closest to: their family. They are moving around the region almost in an isolation bubble, though it is likely they are not physically alone. Of course, during the pandemic, this traveling is not possible.

We all know that it can be very lonely at the top. At least in middle-management, you can go for lunch or a coffee break with the people you work with and share what's going on in your life. It can be far more difficult higher up. Simply because there are less of you at that level and also since you don't share the same problems as those who work under you and the hierarchy in a company makes it common practice to not share honestly and deeply. In turn, especially when business gets stressful, the leader can feel further and further isolated and alone, which can lead them into a more serious state of anxiety and depression.

Here's how a vice president at a software development company in Singapore described his experience of executive loneliness: "As you get higher and more responsibility gets added into your portfolio, it gets lonelier at the top. As a senior leader, you are expected to know the answers and portray a strong outlook for the team to follow. Another point that exacerbates things is the fact that the key decision-making happens in the global HQ in London, and given the time difference between Singapore and the UK, we are constantly 'online' till late evening Singapore time. As you put more time and effort to lead the team and deliver results, it takes a toll on your family life. We take the family for granted and expect them to understand our situation. But if we continue to keep taking them for granted, it may have serious, irreparable damages to our personal life. I am still trying to strike a healthy work-life balance, but the recent COVID-19 situation has not made it any easier either."

The Numbers

Let's take a moment to look at some of the statistics about depression and loneliness. The World Health Organization (WHO) tells us that around 5 percent of all people in the world are suffering from depression. Another finding by WHO shows that globally, 75 percent of those who need help, don't seek help due to stigma. Stigma is a huge issue, and it's one that I've mentioned already and that we'll return to simply because it is vastly problematic.

More on the terrible power of the stigma: from the keynotes that I give on the topic of executive loneliness, I have received a number of messages from senior executives telling me they are unable to attend these events because of the stigma attached to the topic. They explained that although they may be suffering, they cannot walk into an event like mine, because they cannot be perceived to be suffering. A large number of people don't want to be associated with the negativity surrounding executive loneliness. This is why we have been attempting to put a more positive spin on the topic through campaigns like "Race to an End of Executive Loneliness." Through my research, I also found that 82 percent of executives in Singapore found it difficult to talk about the challenges they face with their bosses, which goes back to the topic of the previous chapter, *No One Talks About It*.

Farzana's Story

Farzana Shubarna is the global director of Collaborative manufacturing at Center of Excellence Unilever. She is another leader at a billion dollar business who has had to fend off isolation and depression at the top. At 46, Farzana is a single mum with two children, who started her journey in operations management in the US. That was more than 20 years ago, when the field was male-dominated. As she explained, "I worked for years with a sense of not belonging. Any challenges with people or machinery or finance, I had to, by default, manage, deliver, and learn on my own. I knew I had to prove myself to establish credibility, gain respect, and have my peers take me seriously."

"I didn't even have any time—or the option—to worry about how lonely I was or how strongly I needed to connect and collaborate. Fast-forward 20 years to the present, and somehow I have always found myself alone at the top." She was the first female director of manufacturing for a leading cosmetic company in the United States and the first female regional director of operations in her company.

"This loneliness has impacted my personal and family life. I could not speak about my struggles and challenges with anyone at work as I was trying to validate my capability and credibility. At home, I was trying not to bring home my work burden. It became a heavy weight on my mind and heart, and I accepted it as a growing pain; a rite of passage," she told me.

Farzana overcame her feelings of depression and isolation, when she left the US three years ago and came to Singapore after being offered the role to lead her company's Asia operations. What did she do in Singapore to emerge from the depression and isolation? Here's what she said: "I actively reached out to connect and build a network of friends in Singapore," which corresponds to *Step 4–Nurturing Healthy Relationships*. She has also tapped into yoga, meditation, and Deepak Chopra to "learn to accept that I do not have to be perfect and my shortcomings make me human," which corresponds to *Step 1–Taking Stock* and *Step 3–Getting Healthy*.

Farzana's experience of loneliness at the top as well as the proactive steps she took to recover from it shows us, yet again, that this is not a rare experience. It is happening to so many of us, though few disclose it to others. And, like Farzana, by taking positive, thoughtful steps, recovery is possible. However, when we don't address the loneliness, it can certainly worsen and become very serious, even tragic, as the next section discusses.

Executive Loneliness and Suicide

At its worst, executive loneliness can lead to a person dying by suicide. While this might sound extreme, you'll recall from earlier that my good friend, colleague, and fellow executive Simon was silently suffering to the point where he died by suicide. And Simon is not the first or only executive to take such a tragic measure. That's why it is critical we include suicide in our discussion of executive loneliness.

A major taboo is the topic of suicide. In 2019, attempted suicide in Singapore was finally decriminalized, as has already been mentioned in this book. Just imagine: before 2019, taking your daughter to a clinic or a therapist because she had attempted suicide, could be reported and recorded as a crime. Thankfully, this is no longer the case, and we are now able to move forward. The Samaritans, a cause I currently volunteer for, are spearheading a movement to remove much of the stigma surrounding the issue of suicide and mental illness.

How common is suicide? Globally, someone dies from suicide every 40 seconds. That's around 2,200 people every day. At the time of writing, we are being bombarded with statistics about the coronavirus pandemic, but these figures are still dwarfed by the numbers associated with depression.

Here are a few more sobering stats relating to suicide:

- In 2018, the number of deaths related to suicide rose by 10 percent.
- In 2019, in New York City, there were 10 suicides in the NYPD alone.
- In Australia, suicide remains the leading cause of death for people aged between 15 and 44.

The world is currently facing a mental health epidemic with many of those affected suffering in isolation. In the next decade, this could very well become a pandemic.

What does depression and loneliness cost society? Singapore currently spends US$3.1 billion on stress-related illnesses annually. This amounts to 18 percent of Singapore's yearly medical costs. Around 80 percent of Singaporeans live in an "always-on" culture, and 91 percent are suffering from stress. This is a high cost to pay, and it is likely to grow. That's yet another reason we need to recognize and address executive loneliness.

Five Warning Signs of Executive Loneliness

Mental health disorders can be just as dangerous as physical illnesses, but they are not always as easy to detect. Depression can affect anyone, regardless of age or job seniority, but it manifests in different ways. Watch out for these five danger signs in yourself or a colleague to try to determine your/their mental health status and whether some intervention is needed:

1. Intense Feelings of Anxiety and Insecurity

Executives experiencing mental distress may harbor unwarranted suspicions that their employer will fire them at any moment. Or they may turn down new opportunities despite being qualified, because they do not feel capable enough.

2. Distrust of Colleagues

Overly stressed executives may imagine colleagues gossiping about them behind their backs and worry about being back-stabbed.

3. Isolation

Sudden withdrawal from social interaction is a definite red flag. Individuals may no longer reach out to friends and family as often as before, which can reinforce feelings of isolation and self-doubt.

4. Addiction and Dependence on Substances

Corporate leaders may drink or smoke to socialize or relax, but the overuse of such substances to cope with stress may result in poorer health and sleep quality, and lead to a vicious circle of more stress and mental unrest.

5. Recurring Thoughts About Death or Suicide

A sense of impending doom can also compel individuals to give away their prized possessions and make end-of-life plans when they are physically healthy. Immediate psychiatric help is advised when the situation deteriorates to this stage.

It is advisable to consult a qualified medical professional for any psychological condition that may be of concern.

The next chapter continues our discussion of how executive loneliness can play out. In it, we look at the not uncommon phenomenon of "smiling depression".

Smiling Depression

Dr Geraldine Tan, the principal psychologist and director of The Therapy Room, who sees many C-suite professionals at her clinic, has observed that executive loneliness leads to varying degrees of depression, which can manifest differently. Dr Tan explained: "There is functioning depression and there is also 'smiling' depression. In functioning depression, a patient is able to carry out his work, but may be quieter and exhibit a constantly low mood level which can last for months. In smiling depression, people work hard to hide their pain. Often, you may mistake them for leading a normal life until they open up to you. Only within the confines of a doctor's consulting room might such patients reveal their pain and begin to emote, which is the first tentative step towards recovery. My patients come to me when it gets too painful to bear. Confiding, crying, or just talking about the problem is a huge release for them, and that process can even save their lives."

The following is how Maureen, who was introduced earlier, experienced her executive loneliness and smiling depression. As you read, consider how her experience resonates with you:

I had been struggling with an operation a few years before that disfigured my face, which made me insecure in a new marriage, which in a perverted way made me take out my anger at my husband, daring him to leave me. The permanent disfigurement made me withdraw from everybody and everything, and I spiraled down quickly. I went back to work after my medical leave and quickly acquired a prickly armor of being cold and super-efficient. I poured all my energy into work, but every other part of my life was in self-destruct mode, but I hid it well. I got promoted at work—I wasn't popular and was known as being quite bitchy, but I got results and the bosses were pleased. I think this was the time that executive loneliness set in—my persona was not me and I had no friends at work that I was ever honest with. In fact, I also pushed my family, husband, and friends far, far away ... because "I didn't like me, so why would anyone else like me, right?" I couldn't take their rejection, so I rejected them first to protect myself. The sense of being alone was, therefore, encompassing, BUT I was functioning ... I was doing well at work, I had friends that I went drinking and clubbing with, I tried church, I did some charity work, I had manicures and worked out at the gym, I lived in a private condo, drove my own car, paid with credit cards, started investing for financial security, and had two kids who had their own nannies. On the outside, I had it going on ... but I also wanted to be dead ... I just didn't have the nerve to commit suicide. How did I feel? I was hanging by a thread and often couldn't breathe, but still I smiled, laughed, and went shopping, so nobody knew.

A senior executive whom I'm calling "Mario" described his executive loneliness and ensuing smiling depression like this: "With [company name]'s results going downhill, and forecasting having become impossible due to the uncertain state of the engagements, it became a quest for me and my team's survival, both in the project and in terms of how to explain the lack of ability to forecast towards my internal organization, often leading to questions that were either inadvertently inaccurately answered or were impossible to be properly answered and left people wanting. I often felt alone fighting these fights, let alone not succeeding in my commitments beyond the work sphere–family, friends, and so on. About smiling depression, the 'fake it till you make it' approach, I had to keep my head high, and most of the time I did–there has to be a believer and I always looked like one, even when inside I felt angry. Inside, I also felt torn, uncertain, hammered, and desperate for relief."

For me, personally, this is how smiling depression became my norm. I left Sweden, my home country, in 1998, lived in Australia on the Gold Coast, and after that, I lived mainly in Southeast Asia. I moved from country to country regularly. So, the only things my family, relatives, and friends back home would see of me was what was on my LinkedIn and Facebook pages. And I would be home perhaps one or two weeks a year.

It's very easy to put on a good show, especially if when you visit home, you stay at a hotel or only meet people for two coffees and three dinners. Everyone can put on a show, and everyone can put that up on LinkedIn very selectively. What you share on Facebook is whatever you want people to see. You can say whatever you want, and you are building up an image of the way you want to show things, rather than how they are. From the perspective of someone back home in cold and dark Sweden, when you see someone on the beach in sunny Australia on the Gold Coast, or in Asia (of course, you choose the beautiful beach pictures or other exotic settings to share), then the person in Sweden assumes you must be happy and living the most amazing life of your choosing. Yes, it's a selective life.

After building up this image, even you start to believe in it a little—that everything really is so beautiful and great. And, of course, there were many great things along the way, and I've had an amazing life in that sense, but there were also a lot of challenges. I've lived in seven different countries, and every move to a new country was a huge challenge, just finding a new job and being surrounded by new colleagues. Moving to a new apartment in the same city is a challenge—imagine the challenge of moving to a new country where you often have to learn a new language. It's extremely challenging, and it takes time to settle in. So it can be harder than it seems, especially when you're hiding behind a façade. A smiling façade.

And if you don't share the truth about the easier parts of your life, what then about the most challenging parts of your life, like your work? Perhaps you're not used to having honest conversations with your relatives because they live far away, and maybe you get into the habit of never sharing anything in detail regarding what's really going on in your life.

And after moving to a new country, naturally you're making new friends. But you're not going to spill your guts out and tell them what is going on with this and that. And it doesn't matter if you have a partner; they can also be going through a challenging time, so you may feel that you don't want to bother them with your problems. After having just moved countries, it's very hard to just start sharing everything that's going on.

If we're looking at senior executives, then it might be even harder to share what's going on because, as I said, it's lonely at the top. With senior executives, you don't have others at your level to talk to that can understand you and your position. You're also a leader, so it's very hard to appear vulnerable. As a result, in many offices, we put on a smile to hide all the pain that we are feeling inside.

And that was certainly something that I did for a long time. And it was only when I started to really talk about how I felt, that I felt better, which is just what Dr Geraldine Tan, the expert I referred to at the start of this chapter, calls the first step: talking to someone. Let me add that for me to continue to feel better, even after having emerged from executive loneliness about two years ago, I must continue to voice my true reality. This isn't a one-time thing. It's about starting and continuing to emerge from, recover from, and stay out of executive loneliness.

Digital Transformation and Executive Isolation

With so many ways to connect with others digitally, why are people still so lonely? Can technology play a role in reducing our feelings of loneliness, or does technology somehow contribute to those feelings?[1] Research findings regarding these questions are inconclusive, and, of course, how a person uses technology, how often, and even an individual's age, can all play a part in whether technology is increasing or decreasing their feelings of connectedness with others.

In a study conducted by Michigan State University psychologist, William Chopik, PhD, that looked at nearly 600 older adults, it was discovered that social technology was positive for these users. Social technology in the study included email, Facebook, online video calling, and instant messaging. The older participants engaging with these technologies experienced lower levels of loneliness, better self-rated health, and fewer chronic illnesses and depressive symptoms than their contemporaries not engaging with such social technology (*Cyberpsychology, Behavior, and Social Networking*, vol. 19, no. 9, 2016).

However, research of young adult groups found the opposite. For example, a study led by University of Pennsylvania psychologist, Melissa Hunt, PhD, looked at 18- to 22-year olds and found that when they decreased their time spent on social media, they ended up actually reducing their feelings of loneliness (*Journal of Social & Clinical Psychology*, vol. 37, no. 10, 2018).

University of Chicago psychologist, Louise Hawkley, PhD, points out that experts agree that technology is changing the way we're interacting socially, and the difference in its effects seems to lie in how it's used. She went on to say, "Those who are substituting online relationships for real

---

1. *Source: https://www.apa.org/monitor/2019/05/ce-corner-sidebar*

relationships, unsurprisingly, don't see a reduction in loneliness and in fact may actually see a deterioration, relative to people who use online interactions to supplement their face-to-face relationships. For older adults who use Skype to talk with their grandkids who live across the country from them, technology really can improve their sense of connectedness."

Evidence from past literature has associated heavy social media use with increased loneliness. This may be because online spaces are often oriented toward performance, status, and exaggerating favorable qualities—by posting only "happy" content and likes—and they discourage any show of personal struggle.

On a personal note, I cannot recall one time I felt happy and relaxed after I spent time on social media. I either envy some of the locations that people I know are photographing themselves at, or find myself feeling resentful about someone's political views. After a social media session, I feel nervous, and I can easily find myself checking social media every hour or so, just to see if someone commented on my post or comments. Sometimes I find a rude comment from a friend of mine. It could even be one of my friends who lives in another part of the world whom I have not seen face to face for a while. We get along well in person, but now separated and only connected via social media, we seem to feel resentful towards each other. Before we know it, we start to make rude comments on each other's posts. The situation deteriorates over the coming weeks to the point that I either block them or they block me. This is a real scenario that has happened to me and many I know. I am sure that social media makes me feel more stressed, anxious, and even lonely. I am sure this is true for many people.

Why do so many of us, including myself, repeatedly turn to social media on days when it clearly does not make us feel good? I can only see one reason: FOMO, the fear of missing out. But missing out on what? Think about it: so many of our own and our friends' feeds are filled by self-serving garbage, bragging, lying, love, a few cat videos, and lots of loaded political content. How could this possibly be good for anyone's serenity?

A friend of mine, Håkan Lagesson, who is a sound healer and spiritual teacher, is a strong believer that it all starts within. Recently, he relayed to me a story where he noticed that when he wrote a post on Facebook, he based his value on how it was received, how many liked it, what comments it got. If it was well received, he was valuable. If not, he was useless, compared to others. This is why he is absent from social media; not to feed that wolf, to find his inner love. He tells himself that: "I am enough, I am precious, I have a place in this world no matter what others think of me and my posts. It sounds obvious, but I know I'm not alone in these feelings," he says. And I agree.

Technology and Executives

Social networks and technological communication tools were designed to make us more connected as human beings and more efficient as thinkers and workers. But have they succeeded? Or, as I argue, and as is supported by lots of research, are they actually making us more isolated and lonely?

Facebook's stated objective is "to give people the power to share, and make the world a more open and connected place." LinkedIn says its mission "is simple: connect the world's professionals to make them more productive and successful." Slack is a "collaboration hub" that promises to "make work life simpler, more pleasant, and more productive," helping organizations "connect their teams, unify their systems, and drive their business forward." Steve Jobs said Apple's raison d'etre was "to make a contribution to the world by making tools for the mind that advance humankind."[2]

In spite of developers' best intentions, digital tools such as these may be having the opposite effect, leading to fewer meaningful interpersonal interactions, less free time, and increasing loneliness—not least of all at the management and C-suite levels.

Much has been written about how the self-esteem and mental well-being of the young is being negatively affected by social media, instant messaging, and the smartphone, the research behind which I already gave at the start of this chapter. Less thought has been devoted to the ways in which digital communication and social media platforms are affecting the professional and personal lives of more mature users, who are in the prime of their working years.[3]

Lawrence's Observations of the Role of Social Media

One male executive, whom we'll call "Lawrence", noticed quite acutely how social media platforms were exacerbating his own executive loneliness. Here's how he described it:

I noticed that I can feel that I am surrounded by a system with assumed

---

2.   Source: https://www.egnsingapore.com/is-digital-transformation-increasing-executive-isolation/

3.   Source: https://www.peoplemattersglobal.com/blog/life-at-work/is-digital-transformation-increasing-executive-isolation-23757

definitions and measures of success, and I am not meeting them. So much seems to re-enforce this—and not only the soft social media platforms like Facebook and Instagram, but also LinkedIn and other virtual and physical networks. A lot of us move in a professional culture where emphasis is put on your profile and brand and where any crack in your ability to be busy and successful is seen as a weakness and a characteristic that means you run the real risk of being thrown out of the "club". It can seem a person's business standing seems to be less about what the person actually knows and how good they actually are; and, instead, all about how good they think they are and how willing they are to build and keep up a fake success persona. LinkedIn and other professional groups are full of people posting about what they think good leaders should look like along with sycophantic platitudes; whereas the reality is that nice and very competent people rarely show off and boast about themselves in this way. So, their talents often aren't acknowledged without the self-promotion.

Social media has created an opportunity for people to paint a picture of themselves having a wonderful time personally whilst being busy professionally. And because of these unrealistic online personas, people feel they need to carry on like that in the real world. They've built an image that they need to maintain, which means they won't let their guard down and will go out of their way to overcompensate and be positive just to make sure that all the effort that went into those LinkedIn humble brags rings true. And don't let anyone see any cracks! For others, they are so desperate to not have any cracks in their professional persona that they keep smiling and being positive when they're not and until they can't. It's like the online professional persona is something they absolutely have to live up to. And then they can't.

The impeccable, highly crafted online presence: tthose in upper management positions report spiraling pressure to maintain polished online presences, with LinkedIn as the pivotal platform. Executives are expected to post news and craft intelligent thought leadership pieces. They're also pressured to post on company intranets detailing their teams' latest successes. Of course, this causes them anxiety over always having to have something to boast about—when in fact, sales records, innovations, and other newsworthy occurrences take patience and effort to achieve. Thus, leaders find themselves in a devastating, impossible cycle: these time-consuming tasks eat up a leader's bandwidth, preventing them from concentrating on motivating employees and spearheading the initiatives that lead to newsworthy performance.

Always working, always on call: thanks to technology, work follows us everywhere—it's impossible to switch off. As a result, it is difficult to impossible to achieve work-life balance. The situation is acute for expatriate executives at Singapore's 37,000 international companies. Working far from the head office, they are already isolated, and often deal with time differences that result in double-shifts, communicating with colleagues overseas late into the night, and further depleting quality time with family and friends.[4]

A 2019 survey by InterNations found that 25 percent of international hires were planning to leave their overseas postings early, the most common reason cited, at 14 percent, being loneliness. Access to professional networking was named by 30 percent of respondents, as a service they wished their company would provide. While Singapore was rated highly for a sense of "feeling at home", it was sixth globally; expats still said building social networks was difficult. On the issue of "finding friends", Singapore ranked 24th internationally.

Less accurate and more time-consuming: issues are generally solved far more quickly and effectively via verbal dialogue. But during the standard working day, technology is being used instead of in-person communication. We're messaging more, but communicating less. In a 1982 memo entitled "How to Write", legendary ad man David Ogilvy dispensed excellent advice, such as, "Never use jargon words like reconceptualize, demassification, attitudinally, judgmentally. They are hallmarks of a pretentious ass." And another: "Write the way you talk. Naturally." He finished the ten-point tutorial with this admonition: "If you want ACTION, don't write. Go and tell the guy what you want." The advice remains relevant—much can be achieved by getting together, whereas time, energy, and nuances such as body language, are lost communicating digitally. Yet we are increasingly discouraged from meeting in person, due to corporate cost-cutting pressures and the anti-flight environmental movement exacerbating matters.[5]

Instead, we are encouraged to make our communication virtual: emailing, messaging, or video conferencing such as Zoom. (We have also been forced to go online more often since 2020, when the pandemic changed the way we work.) I argue that this reliance on too much virtual communication is not good for business, and it's not good for us. There are well-documented links between isolation and loneliness—which can so easily result from a digitally focused existence—and health issues, including

---

4.   Source: https://www.egnsingapore.com/is-digital-transformation-increasing-executive-isolation/

5.   Source: https://www.peoplemattersglobal.com/blog/life-at-work/is-digital-transformation-increasing-executive-isolation-23757

high blood pressure, heart disease, type 2 diabetes, depression, and early death.

The final part of this chapter explores more deeply this issue of in-person versus virtual communication and the impact on relationships because it is just that significant, especially in terms of mental health.

In-Person vs. Virtual

I think that while people have always embellished the stories of their lives, digital transformation has certainly made things worse. We used to belong more to clubs, associations, and societies, and had a real sense of belonging in person. Now we spend that time on social media, hiding behind our devices instead of going to the local bowling clubs, or whatever it may be. We've somewhat lost a sense of belonging. The recent lockdowns and physical distancing measures to protect us from COVID-19 have amplified this.

I have seen, firsthand, the difference of online meetings as opposed to in-person meetings play out in my support group. We, in the support group, were much closer as a group before the lockdown when we could meet face-to-face. Before the pandemic, a relapse of members engaged in the program was rare, but during the pandemic, I estimate that one-third of the members have relapsed. This is because we seemed to have drifted away from truly connecting with one another when the meetings moved online. What we share in the online environment doesn't seem as deep and honest as when meeting in person. Also, we used to be able to meet for a coffee 30 minutes before or after our face-to-face meetings, during which time we might decide to open up more privately to one member of the group. This does not happen on Zoom.

In 2018, Eric Klinenberg, a professor of sociology, media, culture, and communication at New York University, wrote in *The New York Times* that among the key possible causes of increasing loneliness in modern society was "the rise of communications technology, including smartphones, social media and the internet."

Klineberg argued that while tech companies "pledged that their products would help create meaningful relationships and communities," this has rarely proven to be the case. "Instead, we've used the media system to deepen existing divisions, at both the individual and group levels. We may have thousands of 'friends' and 'followers' on Facebook and Instagram, but when it comes to human relationships, it turns out there's no substitute for building them the old-fashioned way—in person."[6]

Indeed, misunderstandings happen all too frequently when you communicate from a distance. If you suddenly send five or seven WhatsApp messages to someone with no response, it's really hard to know if that person is just very busy and doesn't have time to write back, if they actually had a bad day, or if something else is going on with them. And it's very much up to our own mind, mood, and experiences, as to how we interpret the situation. Relationships can deteriorate easily, and people can build up huge resentments when their communication and relationships rely heavily on the virtual.

Rather than having three or five real, solid relationships, we might communicate virtually with 50-100 people. But none of those interactions reach a deeper level. We don't get to a point of being honest and vulnerable. When Facebook first started, you couldn't have more than 100 friends because Facebook believed that you could maintain relationships with no more than 100 people at a time. And even though it's possible to have many more than 100 friends on Facebook these days, I believe Facebook's original thinking that a person cannot maintain a relationship with more than 100 people at a time, is even over-rated. Most people can't even maintain relationships with 20 people, so 100 people is beyond difficult. On Facebook, you've got people that you're "friends" with, but in reality, you don't even know who they are. That's not a friend.

Depth Over Breadth

In 2020 and 2021, I studied with an International Coaching Federation (ICF) coaching program and in 2021, will become an ICF-certified coach. I took this journey because coaching is about asking powerful and deep questions. Not only to others, but also to yourself. It is also about going slow. And that is something that I haven't done in my life. I've always been focused on going forward, without going slowly and deeply with depth and breadth.

I think that's a summary of today's society. Everything is moving fast and is further sped along by innovations in digital technology. We don't stop and breathe and think before we react to something, especially with so much social media. We respond immediately and not with consideration. I argue

---

6. *Source: https://www.peoplemattersglobal.com/blog/life-at-work/is-digital-transformation-increasing-executive-isolation-23757*

that moving slowly and diving more deeply into a subject, relationship, activity, etc., makes for greater contentedness and overall life satisfaction. Less is more.

Some of the advice I learnt from the support group I attend, was to uninstall some of the social media. To opt out. That way, you simply don't give yourself the option to addictively participate in this disappointing trance. You hear from many people, even celebrities, that they have huge social media addictions. I recently read about Ed Sheeran, who went public, saying when he sold out Wembley for one of his first gigs, it wasn't only alcohol that he was addicted to. He was also addicted to social media. He spent, or wasted, the whole day communicating with more than 1,000 people. Ultimately, he had to uninstall those apps to get his freedom back and start his recovery.

Stop reading social media posts, and you'll never know about all of the negativity and drama that goes on. You'll rid yourself of the negative feelings and be on your way to stopping the loneliness you are experiencing too, because you then set yourself up to engage with real-life people.

Chapter Summary—The 5 Steps

What is executive loneliness?

Senior executives under immense pressure to excel have few avenues to vent their fears and frustrations. In turn, this can cause them to feel isolated. This feeling of isolation, in combination with their feelings of stress, fear, and frustration, can lead to depression, anxiety, insomnia, and other similar dysfunctions. This is executive loneliness. And because the executive is in a high-profile position, they can get stuck in this dysfunctional lonely state, and it can end up being detrimental. Detrimental to their health, their relationships at home and at work, and to their whole outlook on life.

The following characteristics that this section detailed, contribute to and exacerbate executive loneliness:

No One Talks About It

Because of the stigma around mental health issues and executive loneliness, people suffering from it, for the most part, don't talk about it. Not with their spouses, their good friends, their doctors, and certainly not with those whom they spend the most time with: the people at work. And when you don't talk about it, you get more and more entrenched in it. The stress and negative coping behaviors pile up, which then exacerbates the depression, anxiety, and loneliness. Not talking about it further increases their sense of isolation and worsens the anguish.

If you do not discuss what's bothering you and your level of discomfort and suffering, your chances of recovery are lower because you'll be holding on to those things and keeping them close, even though it's likely not your intention. Take a leap of faith, and share your secrets with your partner, a friend, a counselor, or a coach today.

It's Lonely At the Top

We all know that it can be very lonely at the top. At least in middle-management you can go for lunch or a coffee break with the people you work with and share what's going on in your life. It can be far more difficult higher up. Simply because you don't share the same problems as those who work under you and the hierarchy in a company makes it common practice to not share honestly and deeply. In turn, especially when business gets stressful, the leader can feel further and further isolated and alone, which can lead them into a more serious state of anxiety and depression.

Smiling Depression

With senior executives, you don't have others at your level to talk to that can understand you and your position. You're also a leader, so it's very hard to appear vulnerable. As a result, in many offices, we put on a smile to hide all the pain that we are feeling inside. Others will mistake us for living a normal and happy life because of the smile we present to the world. This leaves us further isolated and in pain.

Digital Transformation and Executive Isolation

EEvidence from past literature has associated heavy social media use with increased loneliness. This may be because online spaces are often oriented toward performance, status, and exaggerating favorable qualities—by posting only "happy" content and likes—and they discourage any show of personal struggle. Stop reading social media posts, and you'll never know about all of the negativity and drama that goes on. You'll rid yourself of the negative feelings and be on your way to stopping the loneliness you are experiencing too, because you then set yourself up to engage with real-life people.

Recovery

How do we overcome executive loneliness?

Based on my own recovery experience, consultations with mental health experts, conversations with other executives who have managed to recover from executive loneliness, and relevant research findings and literature, as I see it, there are five steps for either recovering from or totally avoiding executive loneliness. This book itself details each of these five steps:

1. Taking Stock
2. Asking for Help
3. Getting Healthy

4. Nurturing Healthy Relationships

5. Finding Your Purpose

The fact that no one talks about executive loneliness, the fact that the very nature of being an executive equates to loneliness at the top, the common practice of "smiling depression", and the tendency for social media platforms to further isolate individuals, are all characteristics at play in executive loneliness that make it very difficult for both the executive themselves, as well as their friends, family, and colleagues, to identify that the executive may be experiencing a serious bout of depression and loneliness. Thus, the executive taking the needed action to emerge from the loneliness becomes even more difficult.

However, by being aware of these contributing characteristics and also educating yourself about the five steps to recovery, you can successfully emerge from the difficult place to live a happy and satisfying life. It takes some effort, but it is well worth it. This book gives you the tools, practices, support, and inspiration to recover from executive loneliness and leave it behind you for good.

Be Honest

Honesty is at the heart of avoiding falling into the loneliness trap. If you have already fallen into the trap, it is key to breaking free from it. We are not talking about a normal level of honesty, but as I learnt in my support group, we're talking about rigorous honesty here. I'll explain what I mean by rigorous honesty in this chapter.

It was clear to me in my support group that everyone could recover from their alcohol addiction if they were honest. Without honesty, the recovery may be short-term only. If a person is caught behaving dishonestly, it can cause immense harm to their relationships and to both their personal and professional reputations. A person who has recovered may easily fall back into bad habits and telling lies, or not telling full truths, again, if they are dishonest. As they stop being honest with themselves and other people, they start to live in denial, and that allows the stress, anxiety, and loneliness to return. In the particular case of an addict, it will likely lead to a relapse. If friends, family, or colleagues find out about the dishonesty, it can destroy any progress the addicted person has made in rebuilding relationships, and they have to start all over again. Even though I'm telling you about how honesty works to free someone from an alcohol addiction, it works just the same in freeing someone from the trap of executive loneliness, depression, isolation, and anxiety.

Some kinds of dishonesty are more harmful than other kinds. People who are trying to rebuild their life after a mental breakdown need to pay special attention to honesty. Not only honesty in terms of other people, but even more importantly, the honesty, or dishonesty, they have with themselves. The failure to establish honesty at a personal level means very little recovery, if any, can occur at all. Honesty is what leads people into recovery, and it is what keeps them there.

Lying and Loneliness

It's hard to admit we're lonely, even to ourselves. Most people deny that they are lonely if asked. They might even deny it to themselves. That is because there is a social stigma to loneliness. We tend to think it is somehow our own fault or that it reveals some personal shortcoming. Loneliness evokes a particularly vulnerable image: someone living alone with no one around them. Instead, it is essential to acknowledge your own loneliness, connect with others about it, and in this way gain their support, ideas, and words of sincere caring, all of which will help you to move forward and emerge.

When you are lonely, it's easy to focus on feelings of sadness or to fill your brain with harsh lies. For instance, harsh lies like, "I'm unlikable and unlovable, that's why I feel lonely," or "There's something very wrong with me, which is why I'm so lonely," or "I must come off as desperate and lonely, so I shouldn't bother trying to meet new people or connect with old friends." When you stop such negative mind wandering and get honest with yourself, you can get proactive and decrease your loneliness.

Why lie to others or yourself about your loneliness? People behave dishonestly and lie to protect themselves. They fear the consequences of their actions, or they don't want to acknowledge the full extent of disrepair and dysfunction in their lives, so they lie to protect themselves. It is easy to fall into a bad habit of lying, denying, or skirting the truth, until it becomes chronic and part of your natural response. And this bad habit is what keeps you in a state of isolation, mental dysfunction, and loneliness.

Dishonesty can lead to feelings of guilt, and a person who is dealing with too much guilt will have problems discovering and feeling real happiness. In fact, they will feel isolated, which is how loneliness gains a foothold.

Executive, leadership coach, and author Andrew Bryant, made this observation about executive loneliness and the essential role of honesty in overcoming the condition: "This is often an invisible condition. Executives can be lonely at the top but be high-functioning. Coping behaviors, such as drinking and working excessive hours, are perceived as normal. This makes it difficult for the executive to accept that they have a problem or for others to support them. Advice varies depending on the individual and circumstances, but where I commonly start is to invite the executive to be honest with what they are feeling and to realize that this feeling is not unique to them. I share that vulnerability is not a weakness, but a strength. When we can be honest with how we feel, we are more relatable and can help others."

Honesty enables healing for the individual and those close to them. If people continue to be dishonest, then their healing will not be able to happen. If people are attending therapy or seeing a coach, then it is vital that they are rigorously truthful during these sessions. Without honesty, there will be little benefit, if any, from such engagement.

Powerful First Step

Honesty is, indeed, a key element to a happy and successful life. It is, therefore, essential that people develop this moral characteristic. It is common for people to play down the importance of certain lies so they can justify white lies. While telling a lie might be the lesser of two evils in some circumstances, no kind of dishonesty should be seen as acceptable. A powerful first step to developing the characteristic of rigorous honesty is owning up to any dishonesty. To move away from dishonesty, you must first recognize when you have told a lie or have twisted the truth. You have to catch yourself in the moment and correct it as soon as possible, no matter how innocent it may seem. Make an effort to consciously stop yourself— even if you are mid-sentence in conversation with another—and correct what you are saying. Apologize if needed. When you are telling yourself something you deeply want to believe, pay attention to whether you are actually being honest, or if you are, in fact, avoiding what is true in the face of what you wish were true. "Radical self-honesty frees you to live your truth." Owning up to dishonesty can be difficult, but not doing so makes it even harder to live an honest life. If you want to feel happy and free, then you have no choice.

I have found out that developing honesty is like building up muscles: the more you do it, the more honest you become. If you are a person who likes to monitor your progress, then keep a journal or use a mobile app to do so. You are then able to track your behavior and can catch yourself if you are becoming dishonest or self-deluding, as you tend to pay more attention to things that you write down.

Remember, too, that becoming rigorously honest is a practice, and it is okay to make mistakes. In fact, making mistakes and recognizing that is part of getting better. Your goal should be complete honesty, though you may never reach this ideal. The aim is for progress and not perfection, and this is the way to deal with honesty. This means that you constantly aim to be completely honest, but you don't berate yourself when you (necessarily) don't achieve it. Instead, you admit and correct any dishonesty and continue trying your hardest.

Leo's Experience with Honesty

The following is an explanation from an executive whom I'm calling "Leo" who experienced tremendous stress and loneliness. It was by getting honest with himself, his family, and his workplace that Leo was able to get the support he needed and emerge better than ever.

Read how Leo explained the experience:

I had spent almost a decade as a "lone ranger"–being responsible for a number of geographies without direct reporting lines. Very few others were in a similar position, and few lasted for very long before moving along. Although I almost always got along well with others, the breadth of the position and the need to report back into headquarters gave me friendly but shallow relationships. It became difficult to relate my experiences and world to old friends who were busy with their own experiences in Australia, talking about politicians I couldn't recognize and housing prices or parking spaces.

While at times my wife and I became strong friends with other couples, such as executives in Beijing, subsequent moves would leave us separated by time zones and distance, as we moved on to different opportunities. Difficult business circumstances and high-pressure assignments soon led me to work extremely long hours to bring together new business areas, which stretched my energy and time. Even on conference calls at odd hours, I found the time lag of conversations led to me being isolated, or constantly interrupting people, or worse, that I had stayed up until 3 am, only for my presence not to be required at all.

It seemed there was always something more important to work on than my own health and well-being. Seeing a few others lose their jobs in rapid restructuring made me feel quite vulnerable to the same problem. It seemed the solution was to work harder. To cope, I soon sacrificed my health and exercise, and used alcohol to give me emotional energy to tackle difficult projects and discussions while working late into the nights. While I would make mistakes, I was able to take on a heavier and heavier workload, so I actually achieved good business results–dulling the anxiety, lack of sleep, and growing sense of despair.

My family noticed my deteriorating health and increasing stress levels, and suggested that I was probably overdoing it, suffering from depression or anxiety, and should get proper medical help. Around the same time, my boss, who had fortunately followed my progress for several years, noticed one of my mistakes and immediately called me to ask, "This is not you, what's wrong?" He also shared some mistakes he'd made over time, and the importance of being honest about problems and feelings earlier, so as to avoid tensions coming to a complete boil.

Despite my fears, I told him the truth–that while I was totally passionate about my role and work, I was struggling with the role's scope and lack of clarity, the pressure, and the lack of support, and that it had left me feeling very isolated and vulnerable. He made sure I felt safe and took my feedback to his management team to ask for more help and support from other teams to work on high priority projects. He gave me express permission to skip late-night meetings and told me where to focus for a secure, reasonable measure of success and progress.

Now that he's sought out support and engages in a number of practices to stay out of executive loneliness, Leo made the following observation about the role of honesty in his personal and professional life:

I try to be honest about what I can and cannot do–and seek to find others in the same situations and share openly what issues I am having. Often they express the same issue, and we simply agree that patience may be the best path forward. My performance reviews have turned into very open and honest two-way discussions–and my manager also shares his performance in the discussions and what he needs to improve. By removing my wall of defense, I don't have to worry about what other people think of me, as I am trying to give them an unfiltered, unstaged picture anyway, and I am aiming to accept feedback based on the reality rather than the image.

Honesty and Business

Running a business that makes it a point to be honest and responsible is a challenge, and many companies end up taking shortcuts to turn a profit. When you look into these companies, you'll likely discover that honesty is not as important to them as they want you to believe. How hard do you think it would be for a business to build trust among its clients if it isn't honest in its business dealings? In business, honesty isn't only about doing things the right way; it's also about expressing the values on which a company is founded.

Importantly, when the business values honesty, its employees start to value being accountable and responsible for their actions. It is your job as a business leader-boss to create this safe, open environment built on trust, and this has to come from the top—from you as the boss. You have to lead by example. The people under your leadership will then start to trust the business and its leadership.

No matter what kind of organization you run, honesty is one of the most effective ways to establish a work culture that will set you up for long-term success. As a leader, the importance you place on honesty will create the kind of culture accordingly. This culture is then what all your staff will live and breathe, and ultimately what your clients will experience.

I choose, in my role as the co-founder and managing director at EGN Singapore, to build our small team on trust. My staff know that I have an open door and open heart for them. We talk about all our challenges, work- and family-related. I am not shy to tell my staff if I go to see the doctor or my therapist because I have anxiety or feel stressed. I even stick the appointment as official in my calendar for everyone to see. There are no secrets in my team, and for this I am proud.

By having this level of transparency, I am kept out of the executive loneliness trap because there are never any secrets at my end of the street. I play with open cards, so I cannot build up any resentments against my colleagues. They also know that they can speak with me if there is something on their minds; perhaps their own loneliness and struggles. This leads to less conflicts, less arguments, and a warmer working environment in general. I urge you to lead in the same way. Try it, and see how not only will it feel better and be more pleasant for you and your team, but the results you all produce should improve as well.

The next chapter on vulnerability goes hand-in-hand with honesty because it takes vulnerability to be honest and it is honest to be vulnerable. The two work together to keep you out of executive loneliness, but the two also require rigor and persistence on your part.

Be Vulnerable

I have learnt through my brief recovery journey that life is not about winning. It is about showing up and being seen. This is the person I want to be. I want to be able to learn from others but also let others learn from me. I want to write things and create things that did not exist before. I want to show up for my family, my friends, my colleagues, and my community. If this is what I want to do, then there is only one thing I know for sure—I will get criticized and I will get my ass kicked. Courage is a value that I hold, and I, therefore, cannot avoid the consequences, which means that I will get my ass kicked. So, I have to build up my resilience and dare to be vulnerable. If you are a senior leader, I am sure that you also have had to live up to a lot of criticism in your life, so this is likely not new to you.

When I told my friend, Andy Lopata, a global expert on professional relationships, and author of Just Ask, that the book that I'm writing would have a chapter on vulnerability, he reflected: "Why do we feel uncomfortable when we need to be vulnerable?" Andy went on to elaborate that one of the key pieces of advice that he shares with his senior executive clients is the importance of being truly vulnerable. If we let go of the need to look good to our friends, family, and colleagues, and let them know when we are struggling, feeling lost, and simply wanting to throw our hands in the air and walk away, they will then be able to help us to overcome these hurdles and challenges.

Most of us have this fear of daring to admit that we don't have all the answers, and we are scared to ask for help. Senior leaders are particularly at risk of seeing vulnerability as weakness when, in fact, people respect seeing their leaders admit that they don't have all the answers. We want leaders who know how to pool the resources around them to come up with the right route forward, not superhumans who know, and can automatically cope with, everything life throws their way.

I was only able to start my recovery when I became honest with myself and then dared to be vulnerable and to open up to my wife (my second wife). I then dared to open up to the fellows in my support group since they provided a place where I felt safe to share. After having shared my story there for a few months, I was ready to share with other people, and for every person I was completely vulnerable with, I felt better.

I came to the support group for my drinking problem, but it seems like I remain there for my thinking. Removing my drinking privileges came with unexpected rewards, and I want more of this. You have all these people sitting around a table being open and honest in a way I have never before heard. It is a safe space with little judgment, and, therefore, little judgment of yourself. It has made me focus on a vulnerability I often ignored before I found this program. That nonjudgmental environment has taught me to expose the ugly sides of myself; it is freeing and life-changing. After each session of opening up honestly and sharing my biggest secrets, something was lifted from my shoulders. I felt lighter. This gave me the confidence to keep opening up to more people and eventually, after my friend's suicide, to open up even on social media, on the radio, in magazines and newspapers, on TV, and now even in this very book. I don't do this for self-actualization. I do it because, by sharing my character defects and faults, I am working on my recovery. Also, it is my duty to pay back to the society that helped me to get well, especially if my candor can help others to get better.

Vulnerability As Strength

One of the executives that Andy spoke with shared how difficult he finds it to be vulnerable. He knows it is important, but, because of his family situation, he has always had to present himself as strong and in control. Admitting that this isn't always the case is extremely difficult for him.

Andy stresses how we all have people around us who would not only be willing to help but would want to be asked and would take great pleasure in being able to support us. And yet, we hold ourselves back because we are worried about being vulnerable.

When asking senior executives how they feel when they hear another person share authentically and vulnerably, they reply that they see the other person as courageous and strong. Andy asked, "Why is it then that what we see as courage in others, we see as a weakness in ourselves?"

Andy believes that there are two mindsets from which we can approach vulnerability. We can come at it from a position of weakness or of strength. Andy said, "When we are vulnerable through weakness, we see our vulnerability as admitting to our shortcomings and owning up to our failures. The act of sharing vulnerably is seen as defeat. In such circumstances, it is not surprising that it makes us uncomfortable and we seek to avoid that situation for as long as possible."

Vulnerability through strength, however, is a completely different mindset. Instead of admitting defeat, we see our vulnerability as a step on our path to victory. We know what we seek to achieve and believe in our ability to get there. We also know, however, where we are falling short and understand the importance of enrolling other people to support us.

Psychologist Maria Mitcha agrees: "When you are at the top, you are supposed to have all the answers. You cannot expose your vulnerability. You are supposed to be the sovereign god-like figure that can deal with everything." She continues: "... but vulnerability does not equal weakness. To be vulnerable means that I allow people to see that I have my own challenges, that I'm being productive about resolving the negative emotions." Leaders, she adds, need to show that, "to have mental and emotional challenges is part of human existence - it is part of life."

Being vulnerable through strength may mean recognizing that others have knowledge or experience that will help us on our journey. It may present itself as a need to draw energy and new strength from our network to fuel the next stage of our journey. It may provide the validation of our ideas that gives us the courage to move forward. To further demonstrate the efficacy of the executive showing vulnerability, let's turn back to Maureen, a pseudonym for an executive who anonymously discussed with me her feelings about loneliness at the top and how vulnerability was key in her breaking free from it.[1]

Maureen: Turning to Vulnerability for Strength

Maureen has worked as the head of corporate communications in charge of internal and external communications and branding at an international business. She's been in the corporate communications line and in a leadership position, managing small teams for 13 years and counting. Maureen told me, "This topic of vulnerability is something close to my heart. Partly because it's a slow realization that being authentic shouldn't be seen as a sign of weakness in leadership and that it can be profoundly positive. It has a really good impact on the team's performance and on the effectiveness of a leader. And it's something that I've only learnt fairly recently."

---

1. Source: https://lopata.co.uk/vulnerability-through-strength/

Maureen explained that for a leader to show vulnerability, it entails "dropping the façade and dropping any idea of what you think you should act like and how you should express yourself and how you should be seen. It is essentially being yourself, being authentic and speaking from the heart."

Originally, Maureen admitted that, like so many executives, she thought that showing this kind of vulnerability was a sign of weakness and, therefore, was a "no-no". She explained, "As a female executive in a male-dominated industry, I've always felt that you've got to act a bit tough. You've got to wear the power suit to a meeting. You've got to work twice as hard as your male colleagues to get just as far. And you need to know the answers, you can't even make mistakes, and God forbid you cry in the office." However, when she finally dared to be vulnerable to her team and to her boss, she had the complete opposite experience.

How did she show her vulnerability to her team? She started admitting when she didn't know things and started asking for their help. "I found these things really difficult to say at first—*I don't know the best solution to this. I have no idea. Let's find out together. What do you think? I was wrong*—but it's getting easier now. I've found it profoundly freeing as a leader. It's allowed me to drop that control-freak nature. And it can open doors and open horizons, and give new ideas."

To her surprise and delight, Maureen found that when she began admitting her vulnerability to her team, they responded really well. They became freer, happier, bonded more, and were more engaged in their work. "Suddenly, they didn't see me as the scary boss," she said, "and they no longer felt they had to act a certain way and be very careful about what they said to me. It was freeing to them because it humanized me when I showed my vulnerability. It humanizes the boss, and then it gives team members permission to speak up, to speak freely, and to admit mistakes. And then when the leader does this, team members are free to say, 'I think I know how to solve it.'"

She noticed real team bonding happening, and she didn't mean the kind of thing that happens at a mandatory team-bonding activity once a quarter. Maureen noticed that, as a result of her own show of vulnerability and humanity to her team, and the freedom and connection that resulted both amongst the team and between herself and team members, a the bonds among them have strengthened and become longer-lasting. The team is stronger due to the authentic connection that they've established. "We have each other's backs. We understood each other's personal motivations and vulnerabilities, and it made us stronger, and that has had a profoundly positive impact on the team's performance."

Maureen noticed two particular things that happened as a result, which improved team performance. The first was that team members weren't just doing the task at hand, but instead, as she observed: "They would very often go above and beyond their job scope; above and beyond their job description. Because it wasn't just a job anymore. They felt a real bond with each other, with me, and within the team."

The second thing she noticed was that, because everyone started to talk a bit more openly, they could better understand the why of each member's personal motivations, both Maureen's motivations and what was important to her, and each team member's personal motivations. In turn, this had a really positive impact when they collaborated. She noticed: "They cooperated and collaborated without having to be told to do so. They jumped in to help each other. The team dynamics were profoundly changed. These were the really personal things that I found to happen when you show vulnerability."

Andy Lopata's findings agree with the positive after-effects Maureen noticed happening on her team when vulnerability was introduced. As Andy stated: "As we have struggled to cope in recent years with greater competition for jobs, a global financial crisis, and increasing economic uncertainty, people are now beginning to recognize that we have to move towards a more open, collaborative way of interacting with others around us. The dog-eat-dog world of the late 20th century lies, for most people, far in the past, and companies are encouraging their employees to work together more than they have before, breaking down silo-style management systems. Being transparent and comfortable and sharing vulnerability with the right people, in the right way, allows us to enhance not just our sense of well-being but also our creativity, productivity, mental resilience, and the likelihood of achieving our goals."

Maureen also said the following, which aligns with Andy's above comment:

One of the reasons I got inspired by the topic of vulnerability was because of the truth of executive loneliness: as you climb the career ladder, the sense of isolation you feel increases proportionally because you feel more alone, and there is a little bit of a power distance between the team that you manage and having to act a certain way. But what I find now is that the old traditional, hierarchical structures that some of us were more familiar with early on in our careers, no longer work.

The old command and control structures—hierarchical; everything depends on the title; title becomes authority—all that is kind of going the way of the dodo bird. Right now, the new way of working is really more about collaboration and cooperation. And a lot of times, especially now, many of us are working remotely. You have to manage teams remotely, and you have to essentially collaborate a lot more across borders and across teams. You work in agile squads, you work in tribes. You come together for short six- to eight-week sprints. There is a project leader, but that leader doesn't actually have authority over the other people in the squad because they come from different departments.

But what do you depend on? How are you going to move the project along? How do you empower the team and get things done and move along milestones? And if you strip away all the corporate jargon that management and consultants come up with every couple of years about leadership and how to be effective as a leader, if you strip everything away, what exactly are you left with?

You're left with people. Human beings. You and I. What motivates us? Is it logic? Is it the rational? No. Logic makes you think, but it is emotion that makes you act. For example, you know that smoking is bad for you. You know, but why don't you quit? It takes a family crisis like a close family member or your parent passing away from lung cancer because of lifelong smoking, then you quit. Or why do you quit only when your baby is born? You shouldn't be eating deep fried food all the time and soda because you know you're putting on weight and it's really not good for your health. Why don't you quit? Why does it take a health scare for you to really take action? Because it's not logic. It is emotion. At the heart of leadership, it is about getting to your authentic self, and for a team to have good performance, the leader has to start first.

If, as a leader, I remain as a robot—a female executive who's strong and tough, who supposedly knows all the answers—my team will not act any differently. But if, as a leader, you start that personal connection, then you kind of build that to a real connection, then how the team acts, their motivations, and how much they put into their jobs, tasks, and projects becomes so much more. This is because they are acting not just from logic or because the boss told them to and there's a deadline; and it's not because they get a bigger performance bonus at the end of the year. It's because they want to. They want to do well as a team; they want to go that extra mile for the boss. And that has been a real eye-opener for me.

Instead of being a weakness, showing vulnerability was the total opposite. It had a profoundly deep and positive impact on my effectiveness as a leader *and the team's performance. And they were happy. They wanted to stay. I also felt that it was an effective way of keeping talent within the company. These days, a lot of people move every three or four years. Why do you stay at a company? Because of the people. It's as simple as that. There's no management jargon needed there.*

Maureen told me a story of something that happened to her 10 years previously when she had a crisis at her workplace and one of her bosses found her, and she'd obviously been crying. Though she was trying to hide it, she couldn't because it was too obvious from her eyes and face. Her boss's response was to share his own personal experience with her for the first time. "I was completely wowed by it. He was being vulnerable to me. And his advice to me was, 'Maureen, it's okay to be human; it's okay. You don't have to act like a robot and perform like a robot 24-7. It's fine'. And it was profoundly moving."

Maureen told me a story of something that happened to her 10 years previously when she had a crisis at her workplace and one of her bosses found her, and she'd obviously been crying. Though she was trying to hide it, she couldn't because it was too obvious from her eyes and face. Her boss's response was to share his own personal experience with her for the first time. "I was completely wowed by it. He was being vulnerable to me. And his advice to me was, 'Maureen, it's okay to be human; it's okay. You don't have to act like a robot and perform like a robot 24-7. It's fine'. And it was profoundly moving."

Maureen's final words about vulnerability, which are very striking, are the following: "I guess age helps, because I'm in my fifties, so I've been there, done that. I paid my dues. It might be harder for someone a little younger, starting out in their career, to just be vulnerable. And I'm not talking about walking around with a box of tissues, sharing about your boyfriend or girlfriend woes with anyone who will listen, but being your authentic self, essentially."

Since you are now on a journey to either recover from executive loneliness or to just learn to be more vulnerable, I would like to challenge you right away to share something vulnerable about your journey with a close friend, a colleague, or as a post on social media that you normally would not share—whether you feel comfortable or not. As Andy said, "Sharing your journey and the obstacles on your path as a way of helping you reach your final destination involves vulnerability through strength. And with the power of your network behind you as a result, you'll find the journey as a whole so much easier." Be vulnerable and let others know the journey you are on, so that they can support you, cheer you on, and hold you accountable.[2]

---

2. *Source: https://lopata.co.uk/vulnerability-through-strength/*

How to Take Stock

Taking stock is about finding personal happiness and alignment in life. How do we really do that? What exactly is alignment? And why is this so difficult for so many of us?

Recently, I embarked on a profound coach training course to develop myself as a professional executive coach to help others. In addition to the deep self-awareness and skills to become a world-class coach that I gained as part of the training, I am finding the HAPPY™ coaching system, developed by Avni Martin, an ICF professional certified coach, founder, and director of Wasambe Pte Limited and the ICF-accredited coach training program, to be a robust and powerful tool to create this alignment with our internal and external worlds, which, in turn, creates happiness.

5-Step HAPPY™

The 5-Step HAPPY™ coaching system stands to create an alignment between your (1) habits, (2) actions, (3) perceptions, (4) purpose, and (5) who you are as a person, i.e., your needs, values, beliefs, etc. The system is summarized in the five steps detailed below, which is my understanding of the 5-Step HAPPY™ coaching system. For each step, you'll also find associated questions, extracted from Avni Martin's 5-Step HAPPY™ coaching system.

1. Habits

Whether we are executives, teams, or organisations, we are a sum of our **habits.**

Step 1 Questions:

- *What long-term habits would you like to create with these new actions and behaviors?*
- *What will that do for you?*
- *Who will you become? Who do you want to be?*

2. Actions

Our habits are a sum of our **actions**; what we say and do automatically.

Step 2 Questions:

- *What actions would you take if all of your perceptions, inner narrative, thoughts, feelings, and beliefs were fully aligned to create the future you want to create?*
- *What would you do if you knew you would be successful at doing this?*

3. Perceptions

Our actions are directly controlled by our conscious and subconscious **perceptions**, meaning our mindset, thoughts, feelings, and beliefs. Our perception is the key to all happiness. We literally shape our world through our perception because all that we do in our lives is shaped by our mind. To change our world, including our happiness, we must create an awareness of our perception, that silent voice inside that speaks to us about everything in life, including who we are, who others are, our goals, and situations. How do we know which perceptions to change and which to keep?

Step 3 Questions:

- *What is your inner narrative, perception, thoughts, and feelings about yourself or your purpose/goals?*
- *What impact is this perception having on your behavior/actions?*
- *What would it do for you if you could create an alignment between your purpose and your perception?*
- *How willing are you to work on this?*

4. Purpose

Ultimately, our perception needs to be aligned with our **purpose**. Most people are not clear about their ultimate purpose. In ICF coaching, one of the first steps we take is creating clarity about one's purpose, goals, and end objective. We need to know where we want to go and why before we can align our internal landscape, i.e., our perceptions, to help us get there.

Step 4 Questions:

- *What is it that you really want?*
- *What is your ultimate purpose?*
- *How clear are you about this?*

5. Who You Are

Finally, your purpose needs to be aligned with who **you** really are, your identity, your values, and deepest needs.

Step 5 Questions:

- *How clear are you about who you really are?*
- *Who are you?*
- *What is the identity that you want to be known for and remembered for?*
- *What legacy do you want to leave behind? What are your values?*

These five steps and their associated questions you can address in a cyclic loop (1 to 5) or also in reverse (5 to 1). For example, if you want to do the reverse, you can start with (5) discovering yourself and then go to (4) define your purpose, (3) develop the right perceptions, (2) design actions, and (1) deliver on long-term habits to become who you want to be. Or you can start by (1) determining what habits you'd like to change and work from there to consider (2) what actions you need to take, (3) how you need to work on your perception, (4) why this relates to your purpose, and (5) who you really are.

Whether you're starting with step 1 or step 5, for each step's questions, write down whatever comes up for you until you find the answer at the center of your heart. Next, explore what you find for yourself or with a coach. This is how you can take stock of your life, and from there, start creating alignment.

Sometimes, we're too busy living life to take stock of ourselves. We may forget to think about whether we're moving in the direction we want to go and whether we're taking the right steps to get there. We may even forget to ask ourselves what is most important in life as we are working around the clock and neglecting both our own physical and mental health and well-being.

Take Stock, Create Alignment, and Go One Step Beyond

The support group that I belong to goes one step beyond merely taking stock and creating alignment. This group suggests that we launch ourselves on a vigorous course of action, which is achieved by doing some personal housecleaning with a moral inventory. In the most basic of terms, when someone does this kind of moral self-inventory, it offers them a means of admitting to their past mistakes, acknowledging their strengths and weaknesses, and acting on their potential to make a change in the future.

The purpose of this is to determine the root cause of a person's mental health issues and executive loneliness, to identify any weaknesses that may have contributed to their suffering, and to understand their personal strengths that can help support them with their self-discovery and recovery.

The importance of conducting a moral inventory can be compared with the process of a business owner taking inventory of the items they are hoping to sell. When we examine ourselves through the lens of this metaphor of a business that could collapse if an inventory is not taken, it becomes clear how necessary this moral inventory is, because if we ignore it, we could end up spiritually bankrupt.

When I did this moral inventory, it consisted of me completing a written objective assessment of my life, including defects, strengths and weaknesses, and an overarching look at the damage I've caused to people. On my extensive but not impressive list was anger, fear, cowardice, self-pity, self-importance, egotism, self-justification, self-condemnation, guilt, lying, evasiveness, dishonesty, false pride, phoniness, denial, hate, perfectionism, and intolerance, among many others. For too long I had been holding on to my character defects. I was not even aware of them, and I was not working on improving them. Doing this inventory provided me a powerful means of taking stock of myself, making changes, and improving.

Let's look more closely at the part of taking a moral inventory where you assess the damage you've caused to others. This includes anyone and everyone in your life: family, friends, ex-colleagues, and acquaintances. It can be something that goes way back in time, even 15-30 years ago. After all, you could still be walking around with some resentments for someone for something that happened many years earlier. For example, for a previous job you walked out on and you never reached proper closure for.

In my case, I did a lot of consideration about my divorce when I was very unwell. I hadn't sufficiently dealt with it. There was no closure for this divorce. When it happened, I just suddenly asked wife and son to move back to Sweden without really explaining what was going on. I didn't understand myself because I was mentally sick, and they probably couldn't understand what was wrong either. Additionally, because I was so mentally unwell, I wasn't able to adequately communicate during this time. So it was with murky, difficult situations like this, where I had to own up to my defects and get really vulnerable about myself, that I started looking into closely when I started to take stock.

Taking Stock with Support from Others

As my inventory helped me, yours will help you to accept yourself, plan out changes you want to make, and take responsibility for yourself and your actions. For this to work, you need to be honest and take it seriously. As was the focus of the previous chapter, you must dare to be vulnerable to take stock. That's the way you reap the most powerful and accurate results.

To challenge and ensure yourself that you are being as open, honest, and vulnerable as is needed, it's valuable to take stock with the support of someone else. It could be a therapist, coach, group, or trusted friend. For me, I worked with groups and individuals to get the necessary support for me to thoroughly and honestly take stock.

In the support group, you get help from someone else where you go over everything that you might have done wrong in your life together, so you can be ready to make amends later on (something we discuss in a later chapter). This happened for me. But the non-alcoholic can do these steps together with a counselor or a coach.

I also went on to discuss these challenges with counselors because I realized that I needed professional help. I saw a counselor to try to deal with the challenges I had in the past, to go over those with someone who could interpret it all with me. I also saw a family counselor to talk over things that I'd done to my son during the divorce, because he probably didn't understand, at 5 years old, why his mom was moving with him to one country and his father was moving to another, especially when I couldn't even understand it myself.

As mentioned, I started trying to find an expert in every area of my life, reading books, listening to audio talks and podcasts, and if there was a counselor or a psychologist, I would look them up, book an appointment, and ask them for help. You can see a list of experts that helped me with my recovery journey here: *https://executivelonelinessbook.com/page/bonus*

In order to emerge from executive loneliness and stay out of it, you start by taking stock, which means really looking at yourself honestly, deeply, and with vulnerability. You challenge your findings from every angle and tear things apart to find the truth. As already mentioned, it's going to take some serious vulnerability, so review the chapter on vulnerability if necessary.

Chapter Summary—Taking Stock

The first step in emerging from executive loneliness might sound simple, but in fact, it is profound: you must get honest with yourself about what is happening with you. You must get honest, be vulnerable, and take stock of your life to come to terms with the fact that you are in, and likely have been for a while, a very difficult place of loneliness, depression, anxiety, and dissatisfaction. It is easy to push through the difficult feelings, to put on a smile, continue the daily grind, and hope it goes away. But, that's not how it works. In order to extract yourself and find a happy, satisfied life, you have to get real with yourself about the fact you are experiencing executive loneliness.

Below are the three aspects I recommend for taking this first step towards freedom and satisfaction.

Be Honest

Honesty is at the heart of avoiding falling into the loneliness trap. It is easy to fall into a bad habit of lying, denying, or skirting the truth—especially when the truth is difficult, such as accepting the reality of your own executive loneliness—until it becomes chronic. This bad habit is what keeps you in a state of isolation, mental dysfunction, and loneliness. When you are honest with yourself, first and foremost, about your loneliness, then you position yourself to take the necessary steps to free yourself. If you are dishonest with yourself and denying it, then you stay stuck. You must be honest.

Be Vulnerable

Vulnerability is a strength because it allows us to evaluate ourselves honestly and to put in the effort to seek help even if it may feel a bit uncomfortable. Being vulnerable through strength may mean recognizing that others have knowledge or experience that will help us on our journey. It may present itself as a need to draw energy and new strength from our network to fuel the next stage of our journey. It may provide the validation of our ideas that gives us the courage to move forward. Being honest and vulnerable are critical steps in emerging from executive loneliness and staying out of it. And maintaining that honesty and vulnerability is a continual process.

How to Take Stock

Taking stock and performing a personal inventory of your strengths, weaknesses, hopes and dreams, and people in your life that you might owe an apology to will help you take responsibility for your actions, accept yourself for who you are, identify changes you wish to make, and promote self-awareness. In order to be effective, however, you must be thorough and completely honest. You must dare to be vulnerable and take stock. That's the way you reap the most powerful and accurate results.

To challenge and ensure yourself that you are being as open, honest, and vulnerable as necessary to eventually emerge from executive loneliness, it's valuable to take stock with the support of someone else. It could be a therapist, coach, group, or trusted friend.

Don't Keep Secrets or Stay Silent

After you've taken stock of yourself, perhaps with the support of a trusted friend, therapist, coach, counselor, or support group, step 2 is to share what you find. Share your truth and all of its good, bad, and ugly parts. Share it with others in order to get the help, support, and compassion you need to emerge from your loneliness and turn your life around for good. And as was true in step 1, step 2 is going to require you to be very vulnerable. In order to share your whole and true self with others, and get the help you need, prepare to get vulnerable frequently.

Senior executive and founder of her own coaching company, Avni Martin, knows well the difficult predicament you can find yourself in when experiencing executive loneliness, and when vulnerability is exactly what you need to engage with to emerge. Here's what Avni said: "I've experienced that there are times when I'm going through something at a deep emotional level that I have not yet fully processed, and this has impacted my emotions, confidence, and feeling of being vulnerable. At those very times, what I needed the most was to express myself and show my vulnerability to people around me. I felt unable to do this particularly because of the position that I hold in my company [i.e., company founder and head director]. And the very fact that others are looking to me to teach, train, and show them the way. This certainly did create a feeling of isolation and loneliness until I was able to express it [i.e., get vulnerable] to the right people who helped me understand myself and what I was experiencing at a very deep level."

Psychologist and life coach, Dr Glenn Graves, understands that the very nature of a top-level executive is to stay silent, try to figure things out on their own, and not seek help. As a result, executives often experience loneliness that is longer lasting and very difficult. Here's how he explained what he commonly sees:

For many executives, they got to the high ranks of their personal and professional success because they were extrinsically driven. They had parents who couldn't quite understand a B grade report in school when an A was an option. They may grow up surrounded by constant measurements of their performance and success. Competition is a normal thing, and now that they are at the top, the need to stay there or build on their legacy—that becomes the new pressure. Fear of failure or any aspect of an imposter syndrome can interfere with their peace of mind. Any executive or leader facing this feeling will likely draw inward and not share their dilemma with others. They may have issues with trust and asking for help because it's such a foreign concept.

Most executives are so used to figuring things out on their own, that they are rarely the ones to seek out my help first. They will either begin to show signs of stress through excessive alcohol or substance abuse, socially unacceptable behavior, breakdowns in work performance, and/or marital or family problems compounding. When this happens, an attentive boss or colleague, a caring partner, or even an outspoken child can raise the awareness of the problem.

Awareness is the key. Once a person is aware that they are not functioning well, they can and should seek out support. Support can start with family and friends, community-based support, counselling, and even a psychiatrist. It should be mentioned that the therapy does not have to be a long drawn-out process of sharing your deepest, most intimate stories. It can be solution-focused and get to clarity of the problem within one or two sessions, with the potential for major change in as little as one to four sessions.

Alice Wikström, mindfulness and compassion teacher and life coach, echoed Dr Graves' sentiments when she told me, "It's common to wait for crisis, disease, tragedy, or trauma to happen before we seek support, but this makes the road back to mental and emotional health more painful than it needs to be. In my work as a mindfulness-based life coach, I help people face reality before a crisis occurs. My advice is to share how you feel. 'I am the only one feeling this way' is a painful thought that causes unnecessary harm to ourselves, organizations and families. Find someone to talk to; a friend or colleague that you trust, a coach, mentor, or other professional. There is also the common misconception that if we allow ourselves to feel certain emotions, they will be amplified, but in reality, quite the opposite is true. The more we share how we feel, the less burden to carry."

My Step 2

Here's how my step 2 played out. Initially, I didn't ask anyone for help. I shared nothing about what was going on inside of me. I got married to Dona Amelia, my second wife, but I still shared nothing and managed to reach my lowest point just a month into our marriage. I wasn't suicidal, but

I became convinced my health was so bad that I was likely to die soon, so I wrote my will and testament.

For reasons that I don't know myself, but that I'm very grateful for, my turning point came when I got vulnerable and asked for help. For me, this meant I shared with my new wife Dona Amelia how utterly terrible I felt. When I shared that with her, that was a major step in my recovery. In telling her, I got her support, love, and understanding. Exactly what I needed to start to emerge from that pit of loneliness. Dona Amelia's support then gave me the courage to share what I was going through with more people, which, in turn, meant I had more support, love, and understanding.

Having frequented the support group for problem drinkers for a while, my next move was to share my story with the members in the room. And that's step 2—breaking the silence and being honest with other people, because when you open your mouth and share the truth with someone, then you also start to become honest with yourself, especially when you've been so isolated and encaged by loneliness and the mental conditions that come with it.

I certainly was in dire straights suffering from severe mental conditions that came about due to my executive loneliness. It was very hard to know what was right and what was wrong, and what was true and what wasn't. You start to replay everything inside your head over and over. You don't know what reality is anymore. So that's when I started to speak up and share how I felt. I mentioned it to my wife, and I shared at the meetings. In speaking and sharing my truth, I took it out of darkness and into the light. I started asking for help, which launched me on my journey to recovery.

I remember feeling much better every time I shared my story about what had happened and more of my truth was uncovered. Every day, I was waking up feeling that there were more things I needed to share, more things that I'd kept secret and remained silent about toward my family and everyone else around me. So, I decided to speak up to get it out there, which would give me the help I needed. I started to be honest with my colleagues, I started to apologize, and I broke my silence.

At this point I'd given up alcohol and also started working on the physical health-related steps around diet, exercise, and sleep, and I'd started step 1 about taking inventory. But the main point here was I really began speaking up. It was incredibly powerful and rewarding. I expect the same positive effects to happen for you too.

More Impetus to Speak Up and Get Help

As this journey went on and I kept on seeking and finding help by speaking up, that's when, unexpectedly, my colleague and friend Simon died by suicide. We were all shocked and surprised, and we really didn't know what had happened. Simon seemed very happy. No one could believe that he had been suffering so acutely in silence. Simon's suicide was the ultimate shock for me, and forced me to realize just how imperative it was to speak up and get help, for me and for others like me and Simon who were caught in extreme executive loneliness.

It was upon hearing of Simon's needless, tragic suicide that I decided not only to speak to the people around me in a confidential setting about what was happening to me, but also to widen my audience when I spoke up to get help. I decided to post about my horrific experience with executive loneliness on social media. Soon after, I was invited for a radio interview. There were magazines that also wanted to interview me because of my job at EGN (Executives' Global Network) in Singapore. So, I went from speaking up for the first time to speaking frequently to much greater numbers of people, both to get help for myself and to alert others to the existence of executive loneliness. I also hoped to inspire others to take stock of themselves to figure out if they've sunk into that hole, and whether they also need to speak up to climb out.

It was on live radio, after sharing my and Simon's stories, that I was asked to analyze the difference between Simon and me, and why I was alive and why Simon wasn't. I said that the difference was very thin between life and death. The difference, in my case, was that I started to speak up because the pain was coming to bursting points in me. And while I hadn't reached the suicidal stage yet, it might have just been another day or two before I would have been there also. I said that something similar might've been what was going on inside Simon. Because he didn't speak up, he didn't get any relief from it. He didn't speak to anybody that I know of about how he felt.

A senior executive, whom I'm calling "Mario", was under extreme stress and experiencing tremendous isolation and loneliness over a period of almost a year when he was leading a team that was trying to manage a US $30 million project that was going off the rails. As could be expected, Mario was suffering both personally and professionally in a massive way. He understands how "no one talks about it," and even in the face of that, he gave the following advice: "Find someone to talk to that can give you a different perspective, someone to debate day-to-day matters, intended strategies, organizational models, etc., even if things are not in crisis. I am convinced it is much more effective and easy to avoid crises if you have a team of peers that can debate any type of on-going matter in all transparency, sharing experiences and ideas and helping each other to figure out how to avoid getting on a runaway train. Important to note: it should be a person or people that know you and ideally your situation well, and can spend time to debate."

Repeatedly, you'll find that the executives and experts I've consulted and whose views I present in this book reiterate Mario's recommendation: dare to be vulnerable, be honest, and talk about the personal and/or professional struggles you are enduring. You will help yourself and your team. And it might be more than that. You might even save your own life.

If we're keeping secrets and staying silent, then the most extreme cases can occur—like suicide. And at the time of writing, as the world is going through challenging times, it's all the more important that we don't stigmatize our mental health struggles, and that we do share with the people we love what's going on with us. We mustn't be shy about being vulnerable. As Simon shows us, our very life is at stake here.

Ask for Help!

Why are we scared to ask for help, and how can we overcome this? Is it our own self-doubt or limiting beliefs that stop us from asking others for help? What about you—how good are you at asking for help from others? How often do you stop yourself from asking for help because you don't believe that others will be able to help you? Or do you expect that they won't want to help you?

According to Andy Lopata, author of *Just Ask!*, asking for help is critical to breaking out of loneliness. Of course, this is evident from my own story, and it is tragically evident from my friend Simon's upsetting death. As I said in the previous chapter, I'm alive because I dared to speak up and ask for help. As Andy stated, "One of the things that has become clear to me during the many conversations I have had with senior executives is that their loneliness and struggle is often not visible to others. With few external clues, you can't expect people to offer their help and support. They don't know you need it." This is what happened to Simon. No one knew, and he ended up dying tragically through suicide. It is unfortunate that it is all too common after someone has died from suicide, that people say, "We didn't know about it. We had no idea that this was going to happen. He looked like he was doing great." And that's because no one managed to get the truth out of the person. The person didn't ask for help. They didn't say anything.

I ended up speaking up and getting help simply by telling one person: my wife. I told her because I couldn't cope anymore. She was the first person I opened up to and told about what was going on. We talked about what we should do. And speaking to her is what put me on the road to recovery. She got me to talk to one of my friends who had been part of a program, and that person brought me into my first few meetings with the support group for problem drinkers. And from there, I was more confident about telling more and more people about what was really going on in my life. She also accompanied me to doctors' visits, so I'd feel supported even in those settings.

My friend Radu suffered from depression for 13 years. Finally, he broke the silence and shared his struggle in a LinkedIn post he had been trying to write for over a year. That post in which Radu shared intimate emotions not only provided him with the support and help he needed from others, but reading it, it helped me too. I didn't feel alone. His sharing allowed me to move forward.

It's so common to keep these matters secret. The longer you do so, the worse it gets. But as soon as you make your difficult feelings "official", the whole world comes to you with support, love, and care. Radu was overwhelmed with over 100 comments and a lot of private messages. I had a full-page media article in the Business Times on September 26, 2020, and I shared it on LinkedIn. At the time of this writing, the article has received more than 25,000 views, 400+ "loves" and "likes", and close to 100 comments. In addition to this, I am overwhelmed by private messages from people thanking me for being honest, vulnerable, and spreading the word of an important cause filled with stigma. I am now overwhelmed with love, joy, and support. How different would it have been if I were still silent and keeping this secret? Who could have helped me then?

Remember Farzana Shubarna from Chapter 1, the American executive now in Singapore? Here she shares why she found it so difficult to ask for help, at least initially:

When it comes to executive loneliness, it seems to be considered a weakness. Traditionally and classically, the word "leadership" has been contextualized as a masculine attribute. And being vulnerable and acknowledging feelings, like loneliness, is considered a weakness, aka non-masculine and not that of a leader. So no one would talk about executive loneliness openly, and no one had the trust to open up to others about their reality. I also felt that the fear of being judged also played a role in leaders not speaking up about being lonely.

Most of us have a duty to be the hope and strength for others—family, peers, direct reports, dependents of all sorts—emotional, professional, psychological, and financial. So it is almost always that we need to keep our emotions to ourselves because revealing our "weakness" may cause anxiety and nervousness among those dependents. Whenever I changed jobs, as a single mom, I had to be strong and untouchable and a voice of stability for my kids. For my parents and family members, I need to create assurance that I am okay, so they didn't get to see much of the inner loneliness and interfere in my life.

As you'll read in a later chapter, it was only when Farzana dared to be vulnerable and open up to others about what was really going on with her, that she was able to emerge from executive loneliness and stay out of it over the long-term.

Guidelines for Opening Up and Talking

If you want some more concrete guidelines on asking for help, consider what Andy Lopata advises: "You need to identify key people whose advice, perspective, confidence, and experience you most trust. People who you feel comfortable opening up to and whom you don't feel judged by. People who are good listeners and supporters. If you want advice, make it clear what would best serve you. If you just want people to listen and allow you to unload, be clear about that too. Be firm, clear, and direct when asking for help. Identify the support you are looking for and why you are asking a certain person. Give them a specific task that is practical and explain why you've selected them, reassuring them that they are qualified to support you."

People are there to help, and there is help available. There are excellent therapists and doctors out there. In my case, I've found that doing exercise helps me tremendously. Medicine might help too. The point is: get the help you need, and don't be shy about asking for it. People love to reach out and try to help out.

A senior executive whom I'm calling "Seamus" made the following observations about asking for help: "One of my lessons is that it is okay to ask for help. Asking for help is not a sign of weakness. I have also engaged a therapist to help me overcome personal battles with depression. I have also engaged a leadership coach to help me, and I have recently trained as a coach myself, so I find that helping others also helps me."

We need to change our mindset from believing that no one will help us, to firmly believing that everyone will help us because they, as is true for us, feel great when they can support others. Those beliefs are what I now have planted in my mind and why I am reaching out daily to ask for help. Plus, what do you have to lose by asking for help? The worst that can happen is that the person says no. What can you get from asking for help? The rewards are enormous and even life-transformational. This small mind shift—believing that others will help and even want to help you—will change your life. Try it for a day and you will be positively surprised by the result.

In closing this chapter, I want you to think of something that you need help with. Something that you have been sitting on for a long time, but never goes anywhere. Now close your eyes and imagine that there could be some person out there who might just have an answer. Try to think of three different people who could help you with the solution for this. Now immediately send them an email, message, or call them and "just ask".

What If I Don't Have a Drinking Problem?

After delivering my executive loneliness keynotes to various chambers of commerce, business organizations, etc., in several countries, including Australia, the Philippines, Myanmar, Singapore, and Thailand, I tend to receive the same question at the end of my talk:

"Nick, I understand that you had a mental health and drinking problem, and you got a lot of help from a support group for problem drinkers, but what if I don't have a drinking problem? What can I do then about my executive loneliness?"

This is the question that keeps coming back to me, and I want to address it.

In the context of this book, I've only provided practices espoused by the support group that are highly relevant for anybody who's trying to improve their life. Anyone at all. I have not included practices involving addiction to alcohol. I think there's a misperception about support groups for problem drinkers in that people think that it's a club where you're sitting around and knocking drinks out of each other's hands. That's very far from the truth. In fact, most people in my support group have not had a drink for one, five, or ten years.

We work on a multiple-step program in my support group, and only one of these steps is related to alcohol, while most other steps are related to issues pertinent to all people striving to live more satisfying lives. In reality, the group is about finding a way to live stress-free and in harmony with yourself, so that you can accept who you are and the way that you are, so that you don't have to take a drink of alcohol. Alcohol is treated as a symptom of a larger problem, and it's the same way with other addiction organizations. This is why the teachings are relevant to anybody who is struggling in life. It's these kind of teachings from the group that I bring to this book and to those of us who are struggling with executive loneliness.

Because I have included in this book only the relevant steps that helped me progress through the support group program, this book should serve as a tool to help you move forward with your life, as well. In this book, I give you the best bits of the support program that are relevant to executive loneliness, and I also share my experience with fitness coaches, well-being coaches, International Coach Federation (ICF) certification trainers, clinical mental health counselors, psychotherapists, hypnotherapists, and many other executives who have experienced debilitating loneliness and managed to emerge. I also shared my learning journey as I studied to become an ICF coach in 2020-2021. I am now working as a coach, and I love to help others with their recovery journey.

Get Support From Experts

While a lot of support is available in books, Google, and on apps, it can be hard to find out everything by yourself. It can be overwhelming, and many times we don't even know where to start. We might even get lousy advice from our initial internet search, which can put us on a less-than-ideal beginning. In this chapter, I'm going to talk about the importance of getting support from friends and family, from a support group, and from experts so that you get an ideal start.

I've already mentioned Avni Martin, founder of a coach training school and director of training for an ICF-accredited coach training program. She provides support to executives to help them emerge from executive loneliness (among other things), and Avni herself has had to engage resources when she has experienced the mental anguish of executive loneliness. Here's what Avni says about getting support from experts: "It's natural and I don't know anyone who has not experienced feeling vulnerable and lonely. Find someone you can trust who has the ability to help you understand and process it better, like a coach, a counselor, or a therapist. Find the strength in sharing your experience with others and helping others around you to feel more connected and supported."

Friends and Family

We cannot underplay the importance of having a strong social support network. This means that beyond professional experts and support that you hire, you also enlist people in your friends and family group for support. Research has demonstrated the link between social relationships and many different aspects of health and wellness. Poor social support has been linked to depression and loneliness, so it is essential to take care of this.[1]

---

1. Source: https://www.verywellmind.com/social-support-for-psychological-health-4119970

It is in this realm that my support journey began. As I've mentioned previously, my recovery started when I told my wife how I felt and about all the fear, depression, and anxiety I'd been secretly feeling for so long. I told her because I couldn't cope by myself any longer. In turn, with her compassion and supportive listening and advice, I was able to harness the courage to seek out more support, for instance, from the group for problem drinkers and from experts.

Support Group

When you have to confront a stressful life change or a serious illness, you shouldn't struggle alone. A support group can help. As I've mentioned, I was blessed to have the support group for problem drinkers helping me when I was in my initial stages of seeking help. Along with this group came very effective guidance and simple steps to follow. There are many different kinds of support groups out there.

If you are a senior executive, then you can join an organization like EGN (Executives' Global Network) where you share knowledge in confidential peer groups facilitated by a professional chair. In this way, you get support on your work-related challenges. All members need to be approved and sign an NDA to ensure that what is said in the meeting stays in the meeting. At EGN, we call this the "circle of trust". I happen to be the co-founder and managing director of EGN's Singapore chapter. Belonging to a confidential peer group leads to both better mental and physical health, as part of the focus is about achieving that ever-elusive work/life balance. Through our discussions on resilience and stress management, you'll be given the tools to enhance your personal well-being, which in turn will make you a stronger leader.

If you are based in Singapore or a neighboring country, and interested in joining EGN, then fill in this form, and my team promise to be in touch: https://www.egnsingapore.com/membership-form. If you are located in another country, look around for confidential peer groups.

The executive I'm calling "Leo", whom you were introduced to in the chapter Be Honest, engaged with support groups, as well as individual experts to help him emerge from executive loneliness.

Here's how he described that support:

I saw a number of medical professionals, as well as counselors, and found that I had really been using booze as a massive crutch to get through my workload, and the consistent outcome was that it created even more exhaustion, anxiety, and time pressure. However, I didn't know how to deal with this pressure in other healthier ways, and I had long since lost the fitness levels I once had to use exercise as a stress buster.

I joined an anonymous support group for troubled drinkers and was surprised to find the meeting was full of men and women from a range of backgrounds–including plenty of IT executives and professionals like me. I also joined in sessions of a professional executive networking group in Singapore and found that many of the issues those in the group were struggling with were, in fact, exactly the same ones I was struggling with!

Through this, I discovered two things–I wasn't the only one in this situation. And, two, I felt lonely because I was not well linked up to the right networks of people who were in situations like mine. Instead, I had partnered with alcohol and so had some of them instead. So, in working with these two groups, I found practical solutions I could apply in business and came to accept that this was the reality, and I was not "missing something." I also learned steps I could take to change my relationship with alcohol–and to have other mechanisms and coping strategies that would give me the energy and power I needed to look after myself, my wife, and my family, as well as be useful and purposeful at work.

Having been honest with my manager, I could make well-thought-out, reasonable suggestions to the team on what I could and could not do, given the scope of my work and the resources at my disposal; and I could also relate this to experiences other executives had in dealing with similar issues.

Experts

Even with my wife and friends' support as well as that given to me by the support group, I still needed a lot of help from other external experts, many of whom I've already mentioned—for example, fitness and nutrition coaches, doctors, a counselor, a therapist, a family therapist, a running coach, a gym coach, mentors, a book coach, and even psychotherapy and meditation training experts, etc. I built up my own strong support network of experts to help me when needed. Since my case was so severe and a matter of life and death, I had to invest money into my survival. I was also fortunate to have the funds to be able to afford this. Let me tell you about a few of the experts I worked with, so you can get an idea of the kind of focused support that's available out there for you too. You can find out more here: *https://executivelonelinessbook.com/page/bonus*

Fitness Coach—to get my fitness back on track, I hired a fitness coach. His name is Todd, a Canadian based in Vietnam. We worked remotely together. The only thing I needed to get started was a Garmin watch with a heart rate monitor. I installed the Garmin Connect app, the Strava app, and another app that Todd provided me. Next, we developed a training plan for one year. Todd also agreed to help me with nutrition advice. I bought a scale and weighed myself every day, which meant that we could really see the progress. I could see my resting heart rate dropping through the use of the heart rate monitor. Seeing my fitness level improve was a huge motivator for me as well as, of course, seeing my weight dropping step-by-step, until I had lost 20 kilograms. You'll learn more about my work with Todd in the chapters that address *Step 3—Getting Healthy.*

Family Therapist—as I shared in an earlier chapter, I started to see a family therapist to get help regarding my relationship with my son. He was 11 at the time, but when his mother and I divorced, he was only 5 years old. Plus, he now lives in Sweden and I live in Singapore, and we've been geographically separated for the past six years. Of course, my journey in bettering this family relationship isn't over yet, so when something pops up, I'm not shy about asking for help from the family therapist. Let me give an example.

When the COVID-19 pandemic blew up, and it is still in full force at the time of writing, I slipped into a sort of shutdown mode like many other people. I was locked down in Singapore, as were most people locked down in their country in the world. My son was due to visit me in Singapore in April. Unsurprisingly, the flight was canceled, and he couldn't come. Next, I was supposed to be in Sweden in August when he started at a new school. I had long since promised that I would be there for him during his first week at the new school. However, again, I wasn't there due to travel restrictions.

Because of both of those cancelled trips, I found myself quite anxious and depressed. And as I was working on this book, I reminded myself to ask for help. I called up the family therapist that I'd consulted a year ago, and she worked with me again. She helped me create a survey that would help me have a deep conversation with my son, long distance, identifying what he really valued in life. One of the questions was, "What is the best gift you have ever received in your life?" He said, "my computer." We were then able to identify that he loves online gaming, and I found out that his favorite game was *Minecraft*.

I then bought that game on the advice from the counselor. I installed it, I learned a bit about it, and now my son and I are playing *Minecraft* once a week. We also bought him a headset and a webcam so we can see each other when we play. As a result, it's much easier for us to have a conversation because, instead of talking about things that we don't have in common - since he lives in another country - I can finally connect with him over deep conversations that are relevant for him as we play the game. What happens is that he'll take me around in the game, show me what he built and created during the week, and show me the houses that his friends built. And based on that, another conversation comes up about life, and so on. So, I'm conversing through his world, instead of in my world. Thinking that we have to meet and fly around the world just to have a conversation is ridiculous, especially in an age where we have so much long-distance communication technology. I came to realize all this and to find a way to have real connection with my son virtually, by seeking help from an expert.

I have learnt that to keep myself out of the trap of executive loneliness, I can't do it on my own. As soon as I need help, I cannot be shy about asking for it. And that's important learning that I've internalized and that I want you, my readers, to take from this book. Dare to get out of your head and heart with your suffering by asking for help. You'll only be happy you did so, and you'll wish you'd done it even sooner.

We are so shy about asking for help. Perhaps it comes from fear of being let down and the fear that someone will look at us or judge us. But it's not really true. People are naturally happy to help. And many times, if the person you are speaking to doesn't have the answer, they can link you with someone who has the answer.

In the following quotation, notice how the executive whom we are calling "Maureen" described the efforts she put in to ask for help for her executive loneliness from friends, family members, and experts, as well as taking other positive actions that the other four steps encourage:

"I got medical support for my depression, and I acquired more knowledge about the condition. I can now head off an episode before it gets bad. I've been off anti-depressant medication for years now. I have an arsenal of well-being actions; some have become habits. I keep fit, working out up to six times a week, and got myself certified as a personal trainer. I watch what I eat and have more energy than most women my age. I learnt how to be authentic as a leader and as a friend. I accepted the fact that it's okay not to be okay and realized that everyone has their own mountain of issues … I am not special in that way. I keep a daily gratitude journal–eventually it became a WhatsApp chat group with two girlfriends. Each of us records three things we are grateful for daily to share. This simple daily act was immensely helpful in keeping healthy in the head and heart. Despite my very best efforts, my girlfriends from elementary school and my long-suffering husband have stuck around and have my back."

In conclusion, my first recommendation to you if you are suffering, is that you start by seeking out the help of a well-being or life coach, as well as a doctor. You can find a list of experts available here: *https://executivelonelinessbook.com/page/bonus*

Be righteously honest and vulnerable with them, and you will be on your way to feeling better, less lonely, and recovering in no time.

Recharge Yourself by Reading Books

Since I was a child, I've loved reading. It has a calming effect, and it is a great way to get out of my own head and far away from my thoughts. It makes me think of something else other than myself. It has a meditative kind of effect on me. It has for many years been my favorite activity when on an airplane, on a holiday, and before going to sleep at night. For these reasons, many people love reading and reading can act to lift us out of executive loneliness.

Sadly, in the depth of my executive loneliness and depression, my health was not good enough to be able to read a book. I would read a page and forget what it was about. I would read it again, over and over, and I still would not get it. My mind was elsewhere. So, for a time period, I gave up reading. I tried with audiobooks, which I'd used before, but it also did not work. I'd keep clicking on the "return 45-sec" button to listen over and over because I couldn't concentrate and follow what I was listening to. I had to give up this too. Since my health was not good enough to exercise properly either, I was left with working and drinking as my main activities. What a sad outlook. I point this out to show that sometimes executive loneliness can get so devastating that reading is too trying, but still, just as I was able to take some small steps even in my loneliness to eventually be able to engage successfully with reading again and use it as a tool to further lift myself out of the lonely state, I predict you can too.

I was positively surprised when I joined the support group for problem drinkers and I realized that most of the meetings involved readings. Since, by then, I'd started my recovery journey, I was able to start reading a few sentences, and with this my confidence grew. I can remember staggering on some of the words, but with practice every day, I was steadily building healthier patterns, and reading was part of my daily routine again.

It is amazing what an impact small changes like this can make to someone's life. Suddenly, I felt more calm at night, I was looking forward to reading, and I slept well again. Again, I point this out to you to emphasize the benefits of reading and to give you hope that even if you are too entrenched in depression to read right now, after engaging in some of the other steps to emerge from the loneliness, you will gain the ability to concentrate again on reading and utilize it as a tool to help you further emerge from depression and enjoy life again.

For this book, I researched the benefits of reading and learnt that regular reading not only improves your mental health, but also means that you enjoy a longer life than those who don't read. In 2016, researchers at Yale University's School of Public Health found that those who read books have a 20 percent reduction in their risk of death over 12 years, compared to non-book readers.

Reading has been shown to lull our brains into a state similar to meditation, and it brings the same health benefits of deep relaxation and inner calm. Regular readers sleep better, have lower stress levels, higher self-esteem, and lower rates of depression than non-readers.[1]

Reading makes you more empathetic as well. Reading can be a form of escapism, taking you to faraway lands, other time periods, and allowing you to see the world from another person's perspective. Especially in regard to the last thing, reading from another person's perspective, that's how it makes you more empathetic. It certainly reduces stress as well, so it was not a surprise to me that Islam asks its followers to read the Al-Quran, Christianity recommends the Bible, and my support group also has a dedicated book. It is amazing that something as basic as reading, something that we take for granted, can be so life-changing!

As you can tell, I like books and audiobooks. Social media, television, and even news programs, newspapers, and news magazines I don't promote, because I see all of these as outlets for increasing people's stress.

---

1. *Source: https://www.olympic.org/news/how-olympic-medallist-leon-taylor-is-helping-people-boost-their-mental-and-physical-health-during-the-pandemic*

Below are three tips on things you can do to get started reading and reaping the benefits of reading right away:

1. Don't watch TV unplanned; no zapping from one channel to another. If you watch TV, plan for it and watch something meaningful that relaxes you, educates you, or makes you laugh. Spend all the time you've freed up reading instead.

2. Read meaningful books at least 30 minutes, and ideally one hour, each evening before going to bed. It can be books that are in line with your purpose, self-improvement, and healing.

3. Turn off social media notifications and limit your time on social media. Spend all that time you've freed up reading instead.

These small and easy steps will make a big difference in your life over time.

Chapter Summary—Asking for Help

After you take stock and acknowledge your executive loneliness, which is the first step, you are then ready for *Step 2—Asking for Help*. Step 2 entails you seeking out help from a multitude of people, including friends, family members, acquaintances, experts, support groups, and from media materials like books, articles, and podcasts. Let's review the breakdown of how I recommend you go about asking for help in this section of the book.

Don't Keep Secrets or Stay Silent

After you've taken stock of yourself, perhaps with the support of a trusted friend, therapist, coach, counselor, or support group, step 2 involves you sharing what you find. It's where you share your truth and all of its good, bad, and ugly parts. You share it with others in order to get the help, support, and compassion you need to emerge from loneliness and turn your life around for good. As was true in step 1, step 2 is going to require you to be very vulnerable. In order to share your whole and true self with others, and get the help you need, prepare to get vulnerable frequently.

Ask for Help

It's so common to keep difficult mental health issues secret. The longer you do so, the worse it gets. But as soon as you make your difficult feelings "official", the whole world comes to you with support, love, and care. People are there to help, and there is help available. There are excellent therapists and doctors out there. In my case, I've found that doing exercise helps me tremendously. Medicine might help too. The point is: get the help you need, don't be shy about asking for it. People love to reach out and try to help out. We need to change our mindset from believing that no one will help us, to firmly believing that everyone will help us because they, as is true for us, feel great when they can support others. Plus, what do you have to lose by asking for help? The worst that can happen is that the person says no. What can you get from asking for help? The rewards are enormous and even life transformational.

What If I Don't Have a Drinking Problem?

Even if you don't have a drinking problem, the practices I've shared from my support group for troubled drinkers can help you to stay out of executive loneliness and live a fulfilled life. In this book, I only present practices from the group that I find relevant for anyone looking to emerge from executive loneliness, whether they have a drinking problem or not.

Get Support from Experts

It is critical, absolutely essential, in fact, that you get support from friends and family, from a support group, and from experts so that you make an ideal start in your journey out of executive loneliness. We cannot underplay the importance of having a strong social support network. This means that you enlist people in your friends and family group for support. Research has demonstrated the link between social relationships and many different aspects of health and wellness. Poor social support has been linked to depression and loneliness, so it is essential to take care of this.

If you're facing a major illness or stressful life change, or simply the dire need to recover from executive loneliness, in addition to getting support from friends and family, I highly recommend that you join a support group. I benefited tremendously from the support group for problem drinkers that I joined. There are a variety of support groups out there that could help you as well. Look into it. Even with my wife and friends' support, as well as that given to me by the support group, I still needed a lot of help from external experts, for example, fitness and nutrition coaches, doctors, a counselor, a therapist, a family therapist, a running coach, a gym coach, mentors, a book coach, and even psychotherapy and meditation training experts, etc. I built up my own strong support network of experts to help me when needed. I encourage you to build your own support group of experts to aid you.

Recharge Yourself by Reading Books

Read books and other media in order to educate yourself as expertly as possible on various methods, tools, practices, and ways of thinking to emerge from executive loneliness for good. This book is one such tool to help you. I've recommended the titles of others. And when you talk to friends, family, those in your support group, and other experts, they will share even more helpful reading materials.

Eating and Nutrition

We all know by now that there is a direct link between what we eat and how we feel. Poor diets, researchers say, play a role in worsening mood disorders, such as anxiety and depression. However, diets rich in vegetables and olive oil, such as the Mediterranean diet, can improve symptoms of depression and anxiety. After all, there's a reason for the long-standing belief that "you are what you eat."[1]

As I wrote about already in the section *Step 2—Asking for Help*, I recommend that you seek help from experts in your recovery journey. You'll find in this chapter that much of my learning came from specific experts.

My Nutrition Recovery Journey

In 2018, I crashed. I was trapped in the gutter of executive loneliness to the degree that I literally thought I was going to die. I believed that I was so unhealthy that my body wasn't going to make it. Thus, death. In terms of poor nutrition, at that time, I had a very unhealthy diet consisting of too many pizzas, cheese, bread, beer, and wine. I did not eat enough vegetables and did not take the right supplements.

When I removed the alcohol from my diet in May 2018, I also removed many of my poor eating habits. I replaced the beer with soda water, and the wine with fresh-squeezed fruit and vegetable juices. The pizza I replaced with an omelet. I gained some weight at first, since I was eating more due to having my appetite and other senses back.

This is also when I enlisted Todd Gilmore's expert help, as well as that of other experts. We worked remotely, and he could measure my progress since I wore devices such as the Garmin watch with heart rate monitor.

---

1. Source: https://neurosciencenews.com/diet-mental-health-15384/

Todd had me install an app to monitor my calorie intake, MyFitnessPal. It's a smartphone app and website that tracks diet and exercise. The app uses gamification elements such as goal-setting and tracking to motivate users. While it took me a while to get used to scanning the bar code, or manually inserting every single piece of food I was eating into the app, it made me consciously aware of what I was eating.

MyFitnessPal also measured my weight. I weighed myself daily, and I could see the progress. It was exciting, and my competitive nature kicked in. At one end, I ensured that I never ate more calories than I should, and on the other, I always also ensured that my weight was on track with a slow reduction in weight weekly.

To track nutrients, MyFitnessPal users can either scan the barcodes of various food items or manually find them in the app's large pre-existing database. I was very strict with either scanning or manually inputting into the app everything I ate. I also weighed myself on the scale daily. With these measures, I knew exactly where I was going. Todd and I set an initial target of me losing 0.5 kilograms per week, which I achieved. I kept following this formula and lost 20 kilograms in around 40 weeks.

I also read the book *The 4-Hour Body: An Uncommon Guide to Rapid Fat-Loss, Incredible Sex, and Becoming Superhuman*, a nonfiction book by Tim Ferriss. Important learning from this book is that keeping meals consistent is key for fat loss. It might get boring, but that makes the occasional lunch out all the more tasty and fun. Also, this book taught me about supplements. Below, I'm going to share important nutrition learning that I gathered from Tim Ferris's book as well as from various nutrition and health experts. We'll look at the importance of balanced eating, especially in terms of our sugar consumption; essential nutrients for the best mental health; the role of our gut biome in terms of our mental health and how nutrition influences the state of the gut; supplements to take daily; and a nutritious daily meal plan.

Before launching in to the above, I want to include some interesting overall eating advice from my friends Marcus and Sari Marsden, the authors of Fit to Lead. Marcus and Sari advocate conscious eating as a way to gain more nutrition and health in your meals. How they explain conscious eating is the following: "You slow down your eating, instead of rushing through your meals, and you try to stay mindful in the moment of eating."

Balance, Especially In Terms of Sugar Intake

Watching and limiting sugar intake is something many of the experts talk about. When Todd Gilmore talked about it, he explained it in terms of balance, saying: "Any one item in excess is not good, including broccoli or any one kind of fruit, as examples. The next step in eating right is reducing sugar intake. Coupled to this is ensuring that the carbohydrates consumed are low-glycemic carbohydrates. Other notables, sugar should not be necessary in cooking, and sugary drinks ought to be shunned … Another source of sugar is high-glycemic carbohydrates."

Todd goes on to tell why you should limit or avoid carbohydrates, explaining: "When you consume these, the body converts them to sugar in the blood. Excess sugar is then stored as fat. Plus, excess sugar can stress the insulin pathways in the body, thus opening the possibility of a wide variety of other ailments, which can be directly attributed to excess sugar intake."

Chris Richards, the managing director of Asia-Pacific and Middle East at Ultimate Performance, specifically talked about the dangers of eating sugar, whether in the form of food high in carbohydrates or via alcohol consumption, due to our body's release of dopamine. Chris explained: "It is common to turn to poor food choices as 'comfort food' and alcohol when under pressure and prolonged work stress; however, from years of experience working with top-performing executives, when high-quality nutrition is maintained, this has a hugely positive carry-over into work performance and output. We get a dopamine high when we eat foods considered to be treats, often high in carbs. When under stress, we can often crave this as a temporary boost. However, building in consistent positive habits that you can sustain over the longer term will allow you to feel good more of the time."

Alexander Mearns, health practitioner and founder of Levitise, a holistic lifestyle center (of which I am a member of), and a health and wellness speaker who has guided me with my own nutrition, also said the following about the consumption of sugar and its influence on our mental health and the release of dopamine: "When our blood sugar drops below normal levels, we can feel anxious, nervous, depressed, and angry. Bingeing regularly on sugar-filled foods not only causes blood sugar swings and constant dives into low blood sugar territory, it also repeatedly releases dopamine, a 'feel good' chemical, in the brain. This ultimately leads to fewer dopamine receptors and a demand for larger quantities of sugar to feel good. To avoid experiencing the negative effects of blood sugar level drops, it is vital to eat good quality animal protein and fat at each meal and to not skip meals"[2]

---

2. Source: https://www.levitise.com.sg/diet-emotional-mental-wellbeing

Nutrients

Phillip Kelly, a health and fitness specialist and the director of Body Expert Systems, whose expertise I've sought several times noted: "There seems to be a strong relationship between particular nutrients in food and mental well-being. These nutrients include omega-3 fatty acids, folic acid, vitamin D, magnesium, B vitamins, and tryptophan. These are all found in whole foods that make up a healthy diet." As such, here we will look at most of the nutrients that Phillip mentioned. Please note that I've derived the information about these nutrients both from health experts whom I cite, as well as the just mentioned book by Tim Ferris.

Omega-3 Fatty Acids—fats have played a pivotal role in the evolution and development of the human brain. It is no surprise that omega-3 fatty acids are one of the essential nutrients for optimizing brain function and mental health. The health benefits of omega-3 fatty acids are attributable to their anti-inflammatory, anti-arrhythmic, anti-thrombotic, and hypolipidemic effects. They are involved in many physiological processes that are associated with neuroinflammation, neurogenesis, and neurotransmission. This makes omega-3 fats a fundamental nutrient in the development, functioning, and aging of the brain.

Why so much talk about omega-3, and not omega-6 or omega-9 fatty acids? The recommended ratio of omega-6 to omega-3 fatty acids in the diet is 4:1 or less. However, due to all the vegetable oil, trans fatty acids, poor quality grain feed, and chemically-laden animal products consumed in the modern diet, the ratio is closer to 50:1. While omega-6 is essential in the right amounts, most people need to reduce their omega-6 and drastically increase their omega-3 intake.

B Vitamins—this range of vitamins helps with energy production, fighting fatigue and lethargy, improving the health of the nervous system, supporting the adrenal glands' functioning, and support in the production of substances that regulate nerves and hormones. Vitamins B1, B6, and B12, in particular, assist in the regulation of the nervous system's functions.

Good digestion is another benefit of the B vitamins. B vitamins help in proper digestion and healthy production of hydrochloric acid (HCL). B vitamins also help alleviate stress and anxiety. Studies have shown they are beneficial in helping to relieve the symptoms of anxiety and stress due to their effect of lowering serum homocysteine levels.

Cases of depression are growing globally. Folic acid, also known as vitamin B9, has been shown to help treat symptoms of depression and other cognitive conditions. Adequate levels of B9 may have protective benefits for the brain. Folic acid is found in leafy green vegetables, citrus fruits, and beans.

I want to add in here what Alexander Mearns had to say about vitamin B12, as well as vitamin A and vitamin D. He argues that a vegan or vegetarian diet generally lacks these micronutrients that are essential to supporting mental and emotional health. These micronutrients are vitamins A, D, and B12, and minerals like zinc and iron. Alexander stated, "Research has shown that vegan and vegetarians are more inclined to suffer from depression and anxiety than those who include animal products in their diets. That doesn't mean to say that we advocate eating copious quantities of meat, but a little can go a long way. However, for those that are avoiding animal protein completely, they need to be expertly food combining to ensure a full spectrum of bioavailable amino acids in adequate quantities, in order to minimize health issues."

Vitamin D—like folic acid, vitamin D has been shown to play an important part in protecting against depression and regulating mood. This is important, as research has found that:

- The United States found that 42 percent of people are vitamin D deficient.

- Studies in the UK report 27 percent of people have insufficient or deficient levels of vitamin D with 74 percent of people possessing levels below the optimum range of well-being.

- Singapore found that 42.1 percent of participants were at risk of vitamin D deficiency.

- Thailand reported a 45.2 percent prevalence rate of vitamin D insufficiency.

- Hong Kong found that 72 percent of young people aged between 18-26 are vitamin D deficient.

The percentages are astounding! Is it a coincidence that the total estimated number of people living with depression worldwide increased by almost 20 percent between 2005 and 2015?

Magnesium—magnesium plays a significant role in regulating neurotransmitters. It has been shown to interact with and support the part of the brain that controls the hypothalamus. The hypothalamus helps regulate the adrenal and pituitary glands, which, in turn, are responsible for your response to stress. Magnesium effectively helps to calm the nervous system by blocking receptors in the brain and inhibiting stimulative neurotransmission.

High deficiency rates of magnesium are reported, with up to 50 percent of the American population identified as deficient in magnesium. Magnesium is required to metabolize vitamin D, meaning even if people are consuming enough vitamin D, it remains inactive without sufficient magnesium to process it within the body. That's a big double whammy for the role of magnesium.

Tryptophan—tryptophan is an amino acid. It acts as a precursor of serotonin, the "feel good" hormone. The "feel good" hormone regulates mood and social behavior, appetite and digestion, sleep, memory, and sexual desire. Insufficient levels of tryptophan can lead to low serotonin production, leading to depression, anxiety, impulsiveness, insomnia, an inability to concentrate, and irritability. To boost tryptophan levels naturally you can consume foods like chicken, eggs, cheese, fish, peanuts, pumpkin and sesame seeds, and turkey, to name a few.

The above six nutrients are important for helping us develop and support optimal mental health. However, the food and beverages we eat are not the only substances we consume. In the modern day, the definition of nutrition should include the toxins and pollutants our body absorbs from our environment and body products, as our body has to process these substances as much as the nutrients we eat and drink.

There are also many broader relationships between nutrition and mental health. Good nutrition can provide many mechanisms that help you cope with stress, lower anxiety, and provide vitality as well as day-long energy.

To quickly summarize, the best thing you can do to optimize your mental health from a nutritional perspective is to avoid toxins, harmful chemicals, and substances you're intolerant to, while maximizing your mineral and vitamin intake from whole food sources. Your body will do the rest automatically.

Gut Biome

As Alexander Mearns explained to me, "We have millions of beneficial gut flora, which are friendly bacteria living in our gastrointestinal tract that generate 'feel good' substances that support proper cognitive functioning. However, when the intestinal tract is congested with an overgrowth of fungus and parasites, these microorganisms produce neurotoxins that lead to everything from attention deficit disorder (ADD) to depression.

Furthermore, when the gut membrane is 'leaky', meaning there are microscopic holes in the membrane, undigested proteins and toxins enter the bloodstream. This triggers inflammation in the brain, which then results in brain degeneration and symptoms of mental challenges (depression, anxiety, chronic fatigue, and more)."

Phillip Kelly agrees with Alexander Mearns, saying, "The health of your gut biome, digestive system, and overall gut health also has a big impact on neurotransmitter function and, therefore, brain function and mental health." In summary, Alexander and Phillip both argue that if our gut is not healthy, it will negatively affect the production of neurotransmitters, leading to poor cognitive function, low mood, feelings of depression, and low motivation.

I also learned that gut health is essential to improve our digestion and help us feel better. We will actually feel more energetic because our neurotransmitters will be firing at optimal levels, and our metabolism will be supported so that nutrients and energy sources are getting broken down, absorbed, and used by the body in the most effective manner.

So, what can we do to improve the health of our gut? The best thing you can do is not to eat junk food, artificial substances, preservatives, toxins, etc. Also, getting enough quality sleep supports a healthy gut biome. Alexander also recommends "incorporating foods into your diet that can heal the gut and repopulate the digestive tract with friendly microorganisms. Lacto-fermented foods (e.g., organic kombucha, kefir, sauerkraut, beet kvaas) and glutamine-rich bone broth can help heal the gut to repopulate the gastrointestinal tract with good bacteria. It would also be a good idea to stay clear of antibiotics (unless essential), chlorinated and fluoridated tap water, and concentrated sweeteners that can damage favorable gut bacteria."

Daily Supplements

These are the relevant supplements that I take. The app that I use to buy the supplements is iHerb, *https://sg.iherb.com/*.

- *Dietary Supplement Organics Greens Raw Vegan Superfood* - an essential blend of raw green foods, super fruits, sea vegetables, and probiotics with certified total oxygen radical absorbance capacity (ORAC) factor. It is equivalent to four servings of fruits, vegetables, and greens.

- *Fish Oil (100 Percent Fish Oil)* - lowers blood pressure, reduces triglycerides, slows the development of plaque in the arteries, reduces the chance of abnormal heart rhythm, reduces the likelihood of heart attack and stroke, and lessens the chance of sudden cardiac death in people with heart disease.[3]

- *Gaba* - reduces stress, tension, anxiety, confusion, and depression in people under stress.

- *Magnesium* - reduces stress and anxiety.

- *L-Arginene* - in the body, the amino acid arginine changes into nitric oxide (NO). Nitric oxide is a powerful neurotransmitter that helps blood vessels relax, and also it improves circulation. Some evidence shows that arginine may help improve blood flow in the arteries of the heart.[4]

- *LifePak (Nuskin) Multivitamin* - provides powerful antioxidant support to protect cells; supports the immune system, cardiovascular health, and blood sugar metabolism; completes bone nutrition; and provides other health benefits.

- *Niacin* - rregulates digestion, treats pellagra, improves skin, reduces the symptoms of arthritis, and prevents the risk of heart disease, mental health problems, and diabetes.

- *Odourless Garlic* - used for blood vessel disease (atherosclerosis) and high blood pressure (hypertension)

- *Policosanol* - seems to decrease cholesterol production in the liver and to increase the breakdown of LDL (low-density lipoprotein or "bad") cholesterol. It also decreases the stickiness of particles in the blood known as platelets.

- *Probiotcs* - probiotics help balance the friendly bacteria in your digestive system. Probiotics can help prevent and treat diarrhea. Probiotic supplements improve some mental health conditions.

A Nutritious Daily Meal Plan

I try to eat as much real food as possible and avoid processed food. I am also trying to decrease my animal protein intake, both with the environment in mind, as well as for health reasons. For lunch, I typically eat a small piece of salmon, a chicken fillet, or tuna with one to two potatoes and lots of

---

3. Source: *https://creatorconquer.com/the-best-supplements-for-anxiety/*

4. Source: *https://www.webmd.com/heart/arginine-heart-benefits-and-side-effects*

broccoli and cauliflower and other mixed vegetables and salad. I drink soda water as a treat with lemon squeezed in it. I drink a glass of freshly-squeezed grapefruit juice or a shot of apple cider vinegar before the meal to encourage fat burn.

For dinner I eat trail mix–antioxidant cranberry and blueberry and raisin, dried prunes, nuts and seeds–with homemade coconut yogurt as a light dinner, or I eat oatmeal porridge with almond milk.

As for snacks, on the days I exercise, I have a protein shake with soya milk, berries, chia seeds, banana, and one scoop of vegan protein powder. I also snack on carrots, cucumber, and celery. I cut them into sticks and put them on my work desk as a healthy, easy-to-reach snack that prevents me from going to the kitchen to snack on unhealthy items. Carrot benefits include boosting eye health, aiding in weight loss, ensuring bowel regularity, and helping digestion. Carrots also fight cholesterol and boost heart health; lower blood pressure, and boost skin health. Apart from having carrots on my work desk, I also keep some Fisherman's Friend lozenges around, in case I am craving some sugar. They are strong in taste and low in calories. Other snacks may be nut mixes.

I also drink a lot of water and matcha green tea drink–1.5 liters of water mixed with two teaspoons of matcha green tea powder.

I encourage you to download and install My Fitness Pal, which you can find at *https://www.myfitnesspal.com*, and start tracking your calories. The results will blow your mind.

Making Sleep a Priority

Sleeping helps us recover from mental as well as physical exertion. Sleep and health are strongly related. Poor sleep can contribute to poor health, which in turn can contribute to insomnia. I know this was true for me when I was buried in executive loneliness.

As already explained, I was drinking a lot when I was caught in executive loneliness. Drinking is something that causes poor quality sleep, and when it happens regularly, it instills the awful cycle of stress, distress, and poor health spinning. Because alcohol is a depressant, it can help you fall asleep faster, but it also contributes to poor quality sleep later. Drinking alcohol before bed is linked with more slow-wave sleep patterns called delta activity. That's the kind of deep sleep that allows for memory formation and learning. At the same time, another type of brain pattern—alpha activity— is also turned on. This activity doesn't usually occur during sleep. As a result, when put together, these two types of brain activity can inhibit sleep, so it isn't a restorative, high-quality sleep.

Alcohol consumption blocks rapid eye movement (REM) sleep, the most restorative sort of sleep. As a result, you're likely to wake up groggy, unfocused, and unmotivated. This resonates with me, because when I was drinking, I could wake up feeling drowsy even after nine hours of sleep.

Perhaps obviously, it was by stopping drinking that my sleep totally changed. If I would have known how good I would sleep when I stopped alcohol, I would have stopped it earlier. I am now asleep within one minute of putting my head on the pillow, every night. I also don't wake up in the middle of the night having to go and drink water followed by going to the toilet, creating a negative cycle due to the dehydration from the alcohol. I may have one brief toilet break at night, but then I go straight back to deep sleep after a minute. At the end of this chapter, I'll share more of the things I'm doing to help me get quality sleep. Before that, we turn to the experts again to learn their answers to the question: "What is the impact of sleep on mental health?" I introduced all of these experts in the previous chapter, so if you'd like to know more about them, please refer to the previous chapter.

From Alexander Mearns

Alexander Mearns cited the following to explain the role of sleep on mental health:

Sleep is critical for mental health as you mentally recharge during the night, particularly between the hours of 2 am and 6 am. If you're waking up during those hours, then your mental recovery will be impaired. Light pollution, EMF (electric and magnetic fields), diet, hot rooms, alcohol, caffeine, sugar, stress, and poor breathing can all affect the quality of your sleep and how deeply and restoratively you sleep.

From Chris Richards

Chris Richards gave the following response when asked about the relationship between sleep and mental health:

When you sleep, your body restores and recovers from the workload placed on it, both physically and mentally. When your sleep is regularly disrupted due to stress, it can have a negative effect on your mood, performance, and energy levels. As an executive under regular stress, you need to explore ways to switch off, unwind, and recharge, as your ability to do so will allow for higher levels of performance, better decision-making, and more control over your emotions— all important factors in ensuring continued career success.

In addition to stress disrupting sleep, inconsistent food choices and excessive alcohol consumption can also negatively impact your ability to get good quality sleep. Regardless of the reason sleep is disrupted, this can lead to mental health strain and feelings that are not manageable.

Everyone is different, so finding the approach that works well for you to improve your "sleep hygiene" is something that is well worth thinking about. For starters, I recommend that your bedroom be as dark as possible with a controlled temperature to help improve your sleep. The increasing popularity of wearables has made many people more aware of health metrics including their sleep. This in itself is positive to create more awareness similar to how counting the number of steps you achieve each day provides you more awareness on your walking and overall movement. Data shows that tracking sleep improves output in individuals who track it.

From Marcus and Sara Marsden

Marcus and Sara answered, saying the following:

We believe that sleep is the mother of health. Scientists are learning more and more about the regenerative properties of sleep. Sleep is a critical factor in this equation of rest and recovery. Research suggests that poor sleep can cause mental health problems such as anxiety and depression. If you want to continue to learn, grow, and develop as well as experience peak performance, then sleep is a critical factor in your rest and recovery practice.

From Jeff Huang Zhi Yang

Jeff Huang Zhi Yang is physical trainer at Virgin Fitness for Strength, and he was my personal trainer there as well. Jeff said the following about sleep and mental health:

Sleep is the only time where our body naturally reduces its cortisol level, which is the main hormone that causes us to feel stress. Our human body has a smart system where it will allow us to do what we want. So even if we have a lack of sleep, the body will still function as we want it to, more or less. Even still, this will slowly take a toll on us by causing hormone fluctuations, which may result in temperament issues, burnout, and, at worst, depression. With good quality sleep, our mind can handle stress better and we can better handle difficult issues. Without good quality sleep, our mental health can suffer greatly. In modern times, most people's sleep is not ideal, which is also why more and more working professionals are facing issues with their mental health. Also with good sleep, we can make better decisions with food choices. We tend to choose junk food when we are tired and lack sleep.

My Sleep Recovery Journey

As already stated, once I stopped drinking alcohol, my sleep totally changed from terrible to great. Something else I'm doing to ensure I maintain good quality sleep is tracking my sleep patterns. For the last two-plus years, I've been measuring my sleep and watching it carefully in the Garmin app called Garmin Connect. In there, I see how much I slept the previous night as well as the last seven days. If I see that the average is dropping below seven hours per night, I will make it a priority to go to bed earlier to sleep more and reach around seven to eight hours per night on average. I also try to sleep extra long on one night of the week - say eight to nine hours.

The reason tracking my sleep helps me—and so many others—to maintain healthy sleep, is that it forces me to focus on how I'm sleeping. If something gets looked at—in this case, sleep—it gets done. When you avoid something, it never gets considered, addressed, and solved. That's why tracking sleep, as well as your eating and fitness, can help you make vast improvements that can be maintained.

I urge you to get a smart fitness watch or a fitness tracker, such as a Fitbit or Garmin, and start to measure and track your sleep. Follow my advice to make up for a lack of sleep, i.e., if you sleep less than seven hours one night, then make up for it by going to bed earlier the next evening. Continue this until you get the average, which is your optimal sleep—around seven to eight hours per night. You will thank me, because this is a life-changing improvement.

The fact that sleep is not something to be considered a luxury or an extra. It is key to our physical and mental health. Put in the effort to make it a priority, and notice how your whole being will change for the better.

Exercise: The Real Happy Pill

Exercise has always played an important role in my life, or at least when I have felt mentally well. It is commonly known that regular exercise can contribute positively to depression, anxiety, and other mental ailments. Exercise can also make it easier to get to sleep, improve memory, and relive stress. I have found that exercise makes me feel really good - both physically and mentally. It has been the best treatment for my depression episodes and played a major part of my recovery, and it still does today.

As stated in Anders Hansen's book *The Real Happy Pill: Power Up Your Brain By Moving Your Body*: "Is there a foolproof way to reduce stress and anxiety while you boost your memory? Raise your IQ even as you slow down the aging process? Become more creative and train your ability to focus at the same time? The answer is simple: Move!"

I was given this book from my sweet mom and dad to read during my early recovery, and it truly became my "real happy pill". I was dealing with my depression by taking medication, such as lorazepam, to treat anxiety at that time. This medication acts on the brain and nerves, i.e., the central nervous system, to produce a calming effect. I started to get addicted to it after a few weeks. However, as I was reading *The Real Happy Pill*, in which, among other claims, Anders cites some types of exercise including running as useful in treating depression, I was getting some hope that I would be able to stop taking the anti-anxiety medications soon. I wanted to be free from drugs and alcohol and to live a healthier life.

Before I talk specifically about my fitness recovery journey, let's look at what more experts say about the relationship between physical activity and mental health. Again, because these experts were already introduced in the chapter *Eating and Nutrition*, I won't introduce them again because you can find their background information in that chapter.

From Chris Richards

Chris told me the following when I asked him about the relationship between movement and mental health:

Exercise is an incredible way to manage our mental health and, in turn, improve and maintain our health, which is truly the most important thing for us to protect at all costs. Whether this be choosing a form of cardio where you can explore or escape, or enjoying the buzz of lifting weights in a gym, find the form of exercise that you enjoy and that works for you and your schedule.

With so many deadlines and competing priorities professionally, it's important to build time into your schedule that focuses on movement and your health. Creating these habits will motivate you to make better food choices, improve the quality of your sleep, and support your mental health, which, like any form of physical health, is not a fixed state and can change over time. Plus, no one is immune from facing difficulties. Additionally, achieving something positive every day that is 100 percent for yourself and has favorable health benefits, which is what physical activity does for you, has a great cumulative effect on how you view your self-image and confidence.

From Marcus and Sari Marsden

Marcus and Sari answered the question like this:

We believe involving your physical state in your development and journey through life is fundamental if you want to keep developing and growing sustainably. Your physical state can influence your emotional and mental health too. We observe from our clients who don't move their body enough, that they feel more stressed. We also notice those who are physically active have more energy and demonstrate the ability to shift their mood. Regular exercise develops chemicals that support a healthy hippocampus (the part of your brain that supports memory and learning). It releases endorphins and serotonin, the "feel good" chemicals, and increases concentrations of norepinephrine, a chemical that improves the brain's response to stress. Regular exercise can help us to boost our mood, self-esteem, and increase our capacity to lead others too. The key is to make physical activity a sustainable habit and regular part of our life. Exercise is optional; movement is fundamental. Start by choosing a physical activity that you enjoy and something that you'll want to keep doing. Move your body, move your life.

From Jeff Huang Zhi Yang

Jeff cited the following as the impact of exercise on mental health:

With good nutrition and good quality sleep, when you add in exercise, your body and mind will be in great shape! Exercise improves our mood and also strengthens our mindset. During exercise, endorphins increase and it significantly improves anyone's mood, especially when fun is involved during exercise. When you have a lack of exercise, moods are usually dull, and we become more and more lethargic, which brings a lot of negative feelings in as we move less and get lazier. Exercise encourages us to be just like how we behaved when we were kids, running around, laughing, and being happy because that's our natural state. Exercise teaches us that we can do better in life, and simply moving makes us feel better, which will then help our mind to feel more positive easily. As we strengthen our body, our mind gets stronger too!

From Todd Gilmore

This is how Todd explained the relationship between exercise and mental health:

Every major medical association recommends exercise. The benefits are too abundant to list. Exercise can also become a stress source if not placed in the correct context. For example, signing up for an event when you know you don't have sufficient time to train is not good for mental health. Similarly, if your favorite gym or exercise location is a 45-minute departure from the normal commute, the time stress may not be worth the trip. Exercise ought to be convenient and enjoyable to have the most significant benefits.

Tips to enhance the positive aspects of regular exercise include the following: finding the correct workout partners, coaches, trainers, or friends who understand you, your needs, and when to push you and when to have you back off. All of these categories of people may simply be accountability partners. Additionally, the intensity of exercise ought to be 80 to 85 percent past easy. "Easy" refers to simply passing the talk test, i.e., at any point during the activity you can carry a conversation. No fancy devices are required for this test.

Too many people work too hard too often. This may have negative effects on overall physical and mental health as it can lead to greater fatigue. Make exercise convenient. If at all possible, incorporate exercise into a work commute. This is the most time-efficient means of adding exercise to a busy life. Exercise is any activity completed at a steady intensity for 20 or more minutes, and walking is great. Many individuals feel they need to run and run and run. Without correct guidance and understanding, this may only "run" an individual to the doctor's office.

From Jeff Goh

Jeff Goh is a strength and conditioning coach as well as the founder of Jeff Goh Total Fitness. Also, Jeff was my recovery, sports massage, and stretching coach. When I asked him, "How does exercise improve mental health?" this is what he said:

It has been well-researched that the brain releases endorphins, dopamine, and serotonin when we exercise. These are similar to chemicals found in antidepressant drugs, and they make us feel good. For people who are new to exercise or are restarting exercise programs, they might start off feeling anxious and uncertain. However, under the proper supervision of a coach or personal trainer, they will slowly but surely gain confidence in themselves as they become more competent in their workouts and progress towards their fitness goals. Hence, it is no surprise that as they become fitter, their self-esteem also increases, resulting in mental wellness. However, you have to continue pressing on with your exercise and fitness journey to manage your mental health. You should also remember during stressful times that you can go for a run or a swim or head to the gym for a workout to help improve your mood.

Strength Training and Prevention of Age-Related Memory Decline

In the chapters on nutrition and sleep we heard from Alexander Mearns, health practitioner, founder of Levitise, and health and wellness speaker. Here we turn to him again to learn what he has to say about how the regular practice of strength training can assist in preventing or even reversing memory decline as a person ages.

Alexander cites both contemporary research as well as ancient history to provide evidence around this claim. In 2014, there was a study that included 100 participants who were male and female between the ages of 55 and 86, and all of whom had been diagnosed with mild cognitive impairment (MCI). The participants were split into two groups. One group did resistance training twice a week for six weeks. The other group did calisthenics twice a week for six weeks.

Results for the resistance training group were impressive. Participants in that group performed significantly better in the memory and cognition tests. As Alexander stated, "In fact, 48 percent of the whole group reversed their MCI and achieved perfectly normal scores on the Alzheimer's Disease Assessment Scale at the end of the program. The cognitive benefits lasted even 18 months after the study."

Participants in the calisthenics group showed no notable improvements in their mental abilities.

Two years later the same participants were involved in a follow-up study. Again, those in the strength training group fared well. When their brains were scanned, it was found that there was an increase in the size of certain brain areas. However, those in the calisthenics group did not show such size increases in their brains. Hence, this is a significant argument for the efficacy of strength training in not only preventing cognitive decline, but reversing it as you age.

Alexander also cited ancient historical examples that support these findings. As he discovered, "Many of the Greek philosophers, dating back almost 2,500 years ago, insisted that their students engage in regular strength training exercises in order to keep them mentally fresh." Socrates is cited to have said, "No citizen has a right to be an amateur in the matter of physical training … what a disgrace it is for a man to grow old without ever seeing the beauty and strength of which his body is capable." Plato is quoted as saying, "In order for man to succeed in life, God provided him with two means, education and physical activity. Not separately, one for the soul and the other for the body, but for the two together. With these two means, man can attain perfection." Hippocrates, the famous Greek physician, who is a founding figure even in today's modern study of medicine, promoted modifications in diet and exercise to treat and reverse disease in his patients.

Here are Alexander's recommendations for the "how-to" of strength training:

- Use free weights rather than machines because free weights require you to use more muscles, which then means you get more neurons in your brain firing up, which leads to those great improvements in memory and cognition.
- Each week, do two or three strength training sessions lasting 45 to 60 minutes each.

In addition to improvements in the brain, Alexander reminds us that strength training is also effective for those looking to lose weight.

My Fitness Recovery Journey

Having an addictive personality, I tend to struggle to balance things in life. Whatever I get started on I tend to go with to the extremes, and this was also the case with exercise. If I start running, then I stretch myself until I run a marathon. If I drink, then it seems like I am the first person to arrive at the party and then the last person to leave. Therefore, it is little wonder that I pushed myself to complete one of the most extreme long-distance races in the world: an Ironman triathlon.

I completed my first Ironman race in 2014 after having come back from an earlier depression episode and then a second Ironman in Melbourne in 2015. I then had to pull out from my next one in 2016, since I was not mentally strong or physically fit enough at that time, to even make it to the starting line of the race. In 2016 and 2017, when I was in the depths of executive loneliness, I did hardly any work outs at all. I was depressed and replaced my training with alcohol until it became a struggle to simply go for a short walk. I was suddenly 100 kilograms in total weight, which for me is overweight, and not happy.

I was, in fact, feeling miserable and I really wanted to get back into the best shape of my life. I understood, however, that I was seriously ill and I could not make this comeback alone, so I got help. I called up Todd Gilmore, a performance coach at the Endurance Academy, to ask him if he would be my coach and work with me for one year with the target of coming back and completing my third Ironman. Since I'd failed to get myself training on my own for the previous Ironman competition, I needed all the support I could get to make it happen another time. Many friends told me that Todd was the best coach I could find. Todd accepted me as one of his athletes, and I was proud, but a bit scared, and we got started right away. I could now not run away and hide behind any excuses. I had to face it, and knowing my character, if I say yes, then I will show up.

My health target was to be free from the anxiety and depression drugs, to lose 20 kilograms, and to change from hardly being able to walk, to completing an Ironman triathlon just 15 months later. It might have been an aggressive target, but I am a very determined and committed person, and with the hope of *The Happy Pill* supporting me with the notion that training could help me to recover from depression, I was all in for it.

Todd instructed me to use my smart watch to track my activities. I then installed the Garmin Connect app, which tracked all my exercise activities and then Training Peaks, a fitness coach app on which Todd would upload the weekly training plans for me to follow and complete. He would then see how I was performing, and he could adjust the plan accordingly. We started with baby steps, including a daily four-kilometer walk and a short bike ride. Todd then increased my plan, and within one month I started to jog. I could tell that I felt better each day, and I started to reduce the dosage of the anxiety medicine and still felt okay. I felt wonderful after the runs and enjoyed the "runner's high", the natural chemicals released during jogging, which *The Happy Pill* claims improves your health and mood. After three months, I could run a half marathon, and I did not need drugs any longer. Instead, I was relying on a daily exercise routine, the authentic "happy pill" that I'd been looking for. One milestone achieved—I was happy.

Just three months into my recovery and I felt adequately fit and confident again, so I signed up for Ironman Kalmar Sweden to be held a year later. Thus, I had one year to be back in the best shape of my life, ready to swim 3.8 kilometers, cycle 180 kilometers, and then run a 42-kilometer marathon. There was no time for excuses. This big goal kept me focused and helped me discipline myself to get up at 4:30 am most mornings for a swim, bike ride, or a run. This meant a few hours of exercise before having a healthy breakfast, meeting with my support group and then going to work. It made for a great start to the day.

A year later, I completed the race in just under 13 hours, and I was very proud. I completed the race despite having crashed on my bike just three weeks before the race, and I swam the 3.8 kilometers in the ocean with one of my arms taped. I pushed through the pain in the race for a cause much greater than myself, and that was to raise awareness about mental health and to remove the stigma surrounding the topic. I dedicated my completion at the finish line to my friend Simon, who had died from suicide.

At the time of this writing, I am blessed to now have put in two-and-a-half years straight of healthy living with lots of exercise. At the age of 45, I've never been fitter or felt stronger or better. I managed to do two half-Ironman races in 2020, one in Dubai in January, and the second in Thailand in February. I beat my personal best at both.

Benefits Beyond the Physical

It is not just the racing that I enjoy with sports and exercising. It is also the community that comes with it. I'd rather travel with my friends to do races than spend time with them in bars. I also enjoy the training—getting up early most mornings to run or cycle with some friends. What is great is that it also brings me close to nature because we are cycling through nature reserves and jogging in a rainforest or on the beach. How lucky I am. I am so blessed and happy just to write this. I also try to get exposed to sunlight during some of my exercise to get the all-important vitamin D. Jogging or swimming by myself in the morning acts as a meditation for the day. It helps me to breathe and relax.

I have also found that exercise is great as a community builder and for networking. We have the EGN cycling and running club. So we get our networking and exercise done at the same time. The support group that I belong to also has a cycling group. We cycle for an hour and share what is going on in our lives. What a great start to the day!

If you are a senior executive, I recommend you connect with your work team via sport or exercise. It does not matter if you do football, tennis, canoeing, or something else. Just set up a routine to meet interested team members and work out together a few

times a week. You then lead by example and create a healthy culture. They will copy you and do the same with their teams. BINGO! And all the while, everyone is keeping executive loneliness far out of reach.

Recovery and Relaxation

Beyond the recovery that happens through high-quality sleep, there are other practices, namely meditation and breathwork, you can do to cultivate a relaxed and peaceful state of mind and state of body, which is obviously opposite that of depression and stress. After all, relaxation is the enemy of stress.

For me, apart from sleep, I get most of my relaxation from my early morning bike rides through the Singapore nature reserves, followed by a meeting with a support group which also includes being of service. I have started my day as best I can. However, I may not have time for a bike ride, walk or joining the support group every day, so I have had to look for something in addition to these activities. I have also had to find some tools to use during the day.

Meditation

While it was through cycling, joining my support group meetings, and being of service that I gave myself moments of relaxation, which helped me combat the stress, depression, and anxiety I was enduring in executive loneliness, meditating helped me relax throughout the day. While I had never really meditated or believed it would help, I happened upon a good app called Calm that was recommended to me by my support group. Meditation helped—and continues to help—me get my emotions under control and bring me back from the edge of burnout.

Later, I consulted Alice Wikström, mindfulness and compassion teacher and life coach. I reached out to Alice because I wanted to invite her to speak to the EGN (Executives' Global Network) members about mindfulness at one of our events. Alice specializes in emotional and mental health. She helps clients all over the world balance their nervous system, release built-up emotions and stress, and restore the body's energy system to its innate powerful state. Before signing her up to do the session for all the EGN members, I also had a one-on-one session with Alice as my coach, teaching me how to meditate and relax.

Alice explained: "We all experience painful situations in life that can lead us to feel isolated, destructive, and disconnected. It does not have to be this way. Meditation, especially mindfulness, is a powerful tool to quiet the mind and tend to the heart. It helps us look at reality with kinder eyes and less judgment. There are inevitably painful situations in life, but how we choose to relate to and view these situations makes all the difference. Mindfulness meditation helps us face our experiences in any given moment with less judgment and more kindness towards ourselves and others. Over time, this can transform painful thoughts and emotions, and help us view them as opportunities for growth, both on a personal and professional level. As a result, we create new meaningful ways to view and live life."

Alice presented to me the example of one executive she worked with who greatly benefitted from mindfulness meditation, allowing him to emerge from executive loneliness: "He was going through a tough divorce, feeling the grief and sadness of the situation and did not want to share his reality with people at work. This led him to feel disconnected, stressed, and withdrawn, all of which started to impact his work. We began by looking at the reality of the divorce and the pain it caused him by performing guided meditations through the lens of mindfulness. After just a few months of mindfulness coaching, he was able to view his reality as an opportunity for growth, connect more deeply to his child, and show up at work with new-found confidence."

A daily short meditation practice of 10-12 minutes helps me to manage the stresses of the day more easily, and I feel less overwhelmed and less anxious. Mornings are considered the best time for meditation because the mind is less obsessed about the schedule and to-do list for the day, and as the day progresses, the ego begins to run the show.

Dr Graves lent me a brain-sensing headband called Muse which helps people to meditate. If you feel that your mind wanders and you are struggling to get going, and you find meditation has little impact, then this product may help you. It definitely helped me with my meditation and brought more calmness into my life and this is something that is hard to put a price on, at least for me. I became better at calming myself with every ten-minute meditation session I do with the Muse headband. In my first session, a week ago, I was sitting at 4% calm, and in my session today, I managed to reach 80% calm. I feel like a fresh new person or just like I have woken up from a good night's sleep afterward. It is amazing. If you have the funds and are dedicated to improving your calmness through meditation, then I definitely recommend this device. The product I use is called Muse 2, and you can purchase it on this site: *https://choosemuse.com.*

I have also signed up for a series of meditation classes at the Kadampa Meditation Centre, Singapore. Follow me on my LinkedIn page for updates on the progress of this - I will post my results here: *https://nickjonsson.com/linkedin*.

High up on my bucket list is to do a ten-day meditation retreat. I have met with a few of the EGN members who have done this and they say that it is life-changing. You can see more about this here: *https://www.dhamma.org/en/index*

About meditation and accessing a higher power—because I am constantly thinking and feeling and doing, as is true for most of us—I can't access my higher power or the universe in this "doing" state. And it is the "doing" state that is the gateway for anxiety and stress. To find a place for relaxation where I can connect with a higher power and the universe, we must be quiet and still. In meditation, I relax and let go. In meditation, I can practice opening myself to my higher power, detaching from my ego, and allowing the "divine therapist" some time and space to help heal me in ways that I cannot understand, but that ultimately have lifted me from executive loneliness and kept me out of it. With time, patience, and consistent meditation practice, we can develop close conscious contact with our higher power. I believe that this is an advanced aspect of meditation practice.

Breathwork

Dr Glenn Graves described how tension-releasing breaths, something encouraged in certain types of meditation and mindfulness practices, as well as breathwork practice, were meant to ultimately ground a person so that they could begin to gain mental clarity, for challenging faulty assumptions, and allow them to reframe situations toward a positive or at least productive view.

He talked about heart rate variability (HRV) and the training he does with his neurofeedback-focused company Mindful Pathway. By training our physiological response to stress, we can enhance our response by regulating our system. It starts with breathing. With each inhale, our heart speeds up and is said to be in a sympathetic state of the autonomic nervous system. The sympathetic state corresponds to the flight-or-fight response that occurs in anxiety-provoking situations; thus, it is not an ideal state for normal daily life when there is no danger. When we exhale, the heart slows and enters into a parasympathetic state, which is an optimal and relaxed state. Variations in heart rate variability (HRV) tell us whether our body is in a sympathetic state or a parasympathetic state. Slow and steady breaths will take a person from a sympathetic state to a parasympathetic state.

There are variations to explore that each person may find more beneficial. The most common tends to be a combination of four seconds on an inhale and eight seconds on an exhale. In any case, this conscious effort to train your breathing awareness and use it to regulate your body's response to stress will eventually be to your benefit. Dr Graves recommends consistent training through neurofeedback technology or meditation practice on a regular basis to prepare the autonomic nervous system to optimally respond to spontaneous stressful moments.

Dr Graves, who also recently presented to our EGN members, mentioned in one of his talks that when stressed, the amygdala, which is the emotional center of the brain, grows in size as it adapts to the high levels of stress hormones, such as cortisol. A larger amygdala is correlated with more aggression. In his talk, Dr Graves mentioned that even 20 minutes in green space or outdoors in nature could reduce cortisol levels of stress. I know this to be true because there is a clear response in my body when I get on the green corridors of my frequent bike ride.

Vipassana Meditation

One of the EGN members, Richard Cleeve, CEO of Codestream, went to attend a silent meditation retreat and had the following experience. His experience is so inspiring that I've signed up for a meditation class myself.

I had attempted to meditate a few times on and off throughout my adult life, without really giving it the time and commitment it requires. So, when a friend of mine mentioned that you could go for a Vipassana meditation ten-day silent retreat, the only question was how I could carve out the time to do it, having just gone into business with him.

I am not sure what I was expecting, but when I returned from the retreat, I didn't feel any different, pretty much the same self as I was when I'd gone in. But then, a few things happened that I can only put down to going through that experience.

The first was that I was on the phone to my mum for about 20 minutes, and after I hung up, my wife looked at me with an expression of inquisitiveness like she'd witnessed an alien pop into existence on the front lawn or something. For the past few years, I would get very frustrated talking to my mum and, to my chagrin, would get angry with her. On this occasion, though, I was completely relaxed and laughing and joking with her for the whole time I was on the call. That was five years ago, and it's remained that way ever since.

The second thing to happen was that I stopped drinking and smoking. Just like that. The smoking had always bothered me, but drinking was so deeply ingrained into my psyche that not once had it ever occurred to me to give it up. Around two weeks after the retreat, I woke up on New Year's day in 2016, recalled the state I was in the night before, and said, "That's it. No more." The result of that has been better sleep, more time, no more planning weekends around hangovers, and an overall improvement in the general quality of my life.

The third and most important thing to happen was a transformed relationship with my wife. This was partly down to not drinking anymore, but mainly due to an epiphanic moment I had around seven days into the meditation. I was sitting in the meditation hall going through the meditation exercise, and without warning, I experienced a huge wave of emotion well up inside me. It was an overwhelming feeling of love for her, and the realization that all the little things that used to wind me up about the relationship were completely and utterly irrelevant. From that moment on, I have experienced a depth of love and appreciation for my wife that I suspect was in my subconscious, but that I am now completely aware of.

I feel like there is an underlying "something" behind all of these that was always there, but had somehow gotten lost or drowned out in the course of everyday life. And that the meditation clears out all the clutter and nonsense for it to come forward and express its true nature. While it's one thing to try to explain it, I think it is something that can only be understood by doing it.

Another EGN member who tried the ten-day Vipassana meditation is Anupam Yog, Urbanist @ConsciousCities. This is how he explained the experience:

Meditation saved my life, and this isn't an exaggeration. Vipassana (https://www.dhamma.org/), a ten-day silent meditation retreat, taught me an invaluable life skill by simply learning to sit still, observe my breath, and make peace with my thoughts and emotions. Like any skill, meditation must be learned by doing, and akin to brushing my teeth, I don't miss my daily practice. While a ten-day retreat might sound daunting, this is an investment you want to make sooner than later. Over time, I find there are benefits that include increased immunity, improved focus and productivity, and an overall growth in my well-being in all aspects of my life. As I learnt from a fellow meditator: "Don't just do something, sit there!"

My challenge for you: try doing mini-meditations throughout the day– breathe deeply and listen to your breath for 30 seconds, then a minute, and even several minutes. Do this a few times each day. And after each short mindful breathing session, before launching back into what you were doing, take a moment to notice the clearer and more grounded feeling in your mind and body. If you need some guidance and support, you may want to contact a mindfulness coach or simply install the Calm app.

Resources For Getting Healthy

One of the most important things you can do to orient your recovery is to create an action plan to achieve a few clear goals. An action plan, your goals, fitness experts, apps, and other tools like a heart rate monitor, all act as your resources for getting healthy. In my case, I was very unhealthy and lost my fitness, so I needed to get back on track. One way of doing that, as I mentioned in the previous chapter, was to get a coach as a primary getting healthy resource. I hired a fitness coach that helped me to set up a one-year plan. We agreed on what was the overall scope, and every week, my trainer would send me a new plan detailing what I should do that week. At the beginning, it was just walking and getting into the habit of doing that. My coach and the plan we made together were vital resources for getting healthy for me, and there were additional resources as well.

The nice thing about modern technology is that, with wearable devices like Garmin, you can track everything. So if you set up targets, you can make sure that you achieve them. Thus, wearable devices become another helpful resource for getting healthy. You can even set it up in such a way that, if you set a five-kilometer goal for the day, the watch will beep when you reach that goal. But remember to set reasonable goals that you can achieve, and increase them over time. That's what I did.

I walked three kilometers, then four kilometers, then five kilometers, all the way up to the Ironman triathlon event one year later. That's one example of building up to your ultimate goal, but it doesn't matter what your goal is. If your goal is to walk ten kilometers a day, commit to walking every day until you get there. The tools and resources are out there; track your progress over time. If you think you'll benefit from it, you can also hire a fitness coach who can help you set this plan up, along with devices like the Garmin watch I use. This really helped me, and I know it's helping so many other people too. Exercise is so important for your mental state, so be sure to give it a shot. You don't have to set a huge goal; just commit to exercising regularly at first. And as you feel more confident, you can increase your goals.

The following apps worked well for me. They say that whatever gets measured gets done, and by adding some fun gamification elements you will get fit in no time.

Apps and Websites

Garmin Connect for Garmin Sports Watch

https://connect.garmin.com/

I use a Garmin Forerunner 935 sports watch to record my activities. You can record running, walking, cycling, swimming, skiing, triathlons–no matter how you move, you can record your active lifestyle on Garmin Connect.

Strava

https://www.strava.com/

Strava is an internet service for tracking human exercise, which incorporates social network features. It is mostly used for cycling and running using GPS data. Strava uses a freemium model with some features only available in the paid subscription plan.

I use this app to connect with my friends, to get inspiration by looking at their activities, and also to get ideas for new cycling and running routes.

Trainingpeaks

https://www.trainingpeaks.com/

Reach your goals with personalized training plans, accredited coaches, and powerful tools to track your progress. Choose a training plan or coach that fits your life. No matter what your fitness goal is, they have a library of proven training plans to choose from and the option to hire an accredited coach to guide you to success.

I used TrainingPeaks as my platform to work with my fitness coach Todd Gilmore, performance coach at the Endurance Academy. Even though he is based in Vietnam, he was able to upload my training plan in this app, and I followed it so that he could monitor my progress and come back with feedback. You can even select a coach at TrainingPeaks or sign up with Todd. You can find his contact details on my website *executivelonelinessbook.com/bookbonus.*

MyFitnessPal

https://www.myfitnesspal.com/

MyFitnessPal is a smartphone app and website that tracks diet and exercise. The app uses gamification elements to motivate users. To track nutrients, users can either scan the barcodes of various food items or manually find them in the app's large pre-existing database.

I used MyFitnessPal to track all the calories I ate. For a few months, this meant carefully inserting every single thing I ate in the app for it to calculate the calories.

I also tracked my weight in this app.

Calm

https://www.calm.com/

The Calm app is available to download on your phone or tablet. It's filled with hundreds of meditation practices and sleep stories that are written and recorded by some of the top experts. Though it is a meditation app, Calm goes above that.

I use the Calm app to take a ten-minute mini-break in my day, to make a reset to my stress level and then restart work again.

Books

All of these books, I've mentioned already in this chapter. I'm listing them here as a reminder to you of the excellent information they offer on getting healthy:

- *The 4-Hour Body: An Uncommon Guide to Rapid Fat-Loss, Incredible Sex, and Becoming Superhuman* by Tim Ferriss
- *The Real Happy Pill: Power Up Your Brain By Moving Your Body* by Anders Hansen
- *Fit to Lead: Transforming Your Leadership with the 5 Pillars of Performance* by Marcus and Sari Marsden

Chapter Summary—Getting Healthy

Getting your body healthy through healthy eating, adequate sleep, plenty of exercise, and appropriate recovery and relaxation methods will certainly elevate you out of feelings of loneliness, stress, depression, and anxiety, and seriously support you in keeping those difficult experiences at bay.

In the following five ways, we explored what it means to get healthy in the *Step 3—Getting Healthy* section of this book:

One: Eating and Nutrition

There is a direct link between what we eat and how we feel. Poor diets, researchers say, play a role in worsening mood disorders, such as anxiety and depression. However, diets rich in vegetables and olive oil, such as the Mediterranean diet, can improve symptoms of depression and anxiety. It's time to work with an expert to ensure your diet is nutritious and healthy so that through your diet, you are minimizing the potential for executive loneliness and maximizing the potential for living a full, satisfied life.

Two: Making Sleep a Priority

As so well explained by Marcus and Sara Marsden, "Sleep is the mother of health. Scientists are learning more and more about the regenerative properties of sleep. Sleep is a critical factor in this equation of rest and recovery. Research suggests poor sleep can cause mental health problems such as anxiety and depression. If you want to continue to learn, grow, and develop, as well as experience peak performance, then sleep is a critical factor in your rest and recovery practice." Don't underestimate the role of sleep in assisting you to emerge from executive loneliness. Make it a priority today.

Three: Exercise: The Real Happy Pill

Regular exercise can have a profoundly positive impact on depression, anxiety, ADHD, and more. It also relieves stress, improves memory, helps you sleep better, and boosts your overall mood. I have found that exercise makes me feel really good, both physically and mentally. It has been the best treatment for my depression episodes and played a major part of my recovery, and it still does today. I cannot recommend enough that you embark on a fitness program today.

Four: Recovery and Relaxation

Relaxation is the enemy of stress. You can purposefully cultivate moments of relaxation into your day by practicing meditation. Short mindfulness meditations can help you get your emotions under control and bring you back from the edge of burnout. A daily meditation practice of 10-12 minutes can help you to manage a stressful day more easily, so that you feel less overwhelmed and less anxious. In turn, this helps you to stave off executive loneliness. Meditation is a powerful tool for assisting you in battling stress and negativity, and establish a perspective of presence, possibility, and peace in your mind and body.

Five: Resources For Getting Healthy

There are numerous helpful health and fitness books, podcasts, videos, apps, and devices out there to help your fitness journey be more effective, enjoyable, fun, and measurable. Check out my recommendations to empower you for success on this all-important endeavor to get and stay healthy.

The Importance of Healthy Relationships

Relationships are a necessary component in living a good life. Relationships give our life substance and meaning. Relationships are interwoven into our lives. Without relationships, life would be empty and unfulfilling. They define who we are. They bring us joy–and sometimes sorrow. Maintaining healthy relationships, on both personal and professional fronts, is key. Forming and maintaining healthy relationships is critical for those suffering from, or who want to avoid, executive loneliness. Form strong bonds and your circle will be at your side through good times and bad.[1]

Dr Glenn Graves, psychologist and life coach, when discussing the importance of strong and healthy personal and professional relationships, points out, "Any concept or structure of support is necessary for anyone with a heavy burden and heavy task at hand. We are all humans, and if we don't get the support we need, our resources will deplete. The system, the body, and our very spirit can be compromised beyond what can be sustained. There are numerous research reports and real-life examples of those who have succumbed to the pressures of trying to survive in an isolated and sometimes insular world, at the top!

Why wait to be the next example? Executives, men and women, need to feel they are a part of the community they are building. They need to feel appreciated and valued, or at the very least heard and understood. Support groups and professional networking organizations can provide that dialogue, a listening ear, and more importantly empathy from someone who can truly understand."

---

1. Source: https://sg.egn.com/insights/how-to-overcome-executive-loneliness

Healthy Relationships

Healthy relationships are necessary to create bonds, friendships, and provide needed emotional support. Relationships are an effective way of helping someone who is suffering mentally to recover. They are also key to helping a person avoid falling into the loneliness trap. With good relationships, we feel better, and the stronger the relationships, the better we can show up. It is a safe space where we can be ourselves without fear.

Of course, we are all striving for healthy relationships because they bring joy, happiness, hopes, dreams, comfort, and often shared common values built on mutual trust. Healthy relationships come with honesty and encourage each person to share their deepest challenges and issues.

If stress, pressure, or anxiety has led you to unfairly lash out at friends, family, loved ones, and colleagues, make amends and apologize for your wrongdoing. This is something I've addressed already in this book and will address more in a coming chapter. This can really lift a weight from your shoulders.

Toxic Relationships

On the other hand, engaging in toxic and unhealthy relationships can cause immense harm to our mental health. A toxic relationship breeds not only frustration but also conflict, stress, and anxiety. It can also cause an addict to relapse.

Unhealthy relationships consist of damaging and draining dynamics where pressure may be put on one party, such that unattainable goals are set for one person in the relationship. Selfish and manipulative behavior and even bullying and physical, controlling, and dominant behavior can be part of these toxic relationships.

A person in a toxic relationship can feel anxious, frustrated, depressed, and even suicidal. There is a big chance that drug and alcohol abuse could come into play. If you find yourself in a relationship like this, get out of it right away. If you don't know how, see a counselor or a coach and get help today.

Boris's Healthy Relationships

Senior executive "Boris", not his real name, has lived and worked in Japan and now in Singapore. He's experienced some executive loneliness in both places and has been purposeful in building a network of healthy relationships, both personal and professional, and with experts to give him the support he needs to keep executive loneliness at bay. Regarding his executive loneliness in Japan and the pivotal role of relationships in helping him, he said this: "I am married to a Japanese national, and while I have never really confided in my wife about business, when it really got bad, I would get her support also. In general, though, she supported our family very well, so I was always able to focus on my work, and then be 'in the present' with my family when at home. The stability of the home was important in stabilizing my mental ability to keep it together at work, even when it was tough. That got me through some tough days, like when my Japanese business partner had a severe mental breakdown, which I completely missed the symptoms of, and then the Lehman shock when I had to downsize the company by one-third."

When Boris moved to Singapore, his family stayed behind in Japan, so he had to put in effort to build a new support network in Singapore: "It has been about building some friendships or tapping into colleagues I knew from before but didn't know deeply, building networks through places like EGN, doing what I can to network with my local teams, and through COVID-19, trying as much as possible to motivate myself to do different things and keep busy. It hasn't been easy, so I reached out to an executive coach to help me focus on some things and find ways to build more energy. I have also found that regular exercise and a decent social life in terms of meeting friends for dinner and drinks really helps to clear the mind." Notice how Boris's actions to keep himself out of executive loneliness align with the steps I recommend for staying out of executive loneliness. It is no coincidence!

Self Relationship

We also have a personal relationship with ourselves. We wake up with ourselves every morning and go to bed with ourselves every night. We live in our own head all the time—which is why we ought to make it a positive space. The importance of a positive relationship with ourselves cannot be overstated—we are the only ones who will always be around us. For this reason, it is important to put in place positive practices to strengthen your relationship with yourself.

An executive whom we're calling "Seamus" expresses very well the importance of nurturing first the relationship we have with ourselves:

My first experiences with executive loneliness came about through expat placements in countries where I did not speak the language and did not yet understand the work culture and felt that I had to make an immediate impression. Later in my career, I felt very alone despite a significant amount of travel, internal and external meetings, and hour after hour of business updates and strategic reviews. I felt alone as I had no one to discuss these experiences with, as I could not discuss these with my direct reports or the executives in my company for fear of being seen as "weak" or "needy".

I am an introvert who needs quite a lot of time alone to recharge, and more importantly to think and work. I thought that I was doing the right thing by being all things to all people, except myself. Once everyone else was taken care of, every urgent e-mail or phone call was taken care of, I would only then focus on myself and give myself time to recharge. On reflection, I now know that I needed to be more selfish towards my own needs, but what eventually happened is that in trying to satisfy everyone, I satisfied no one, including myself. This was clearly unsustainable and had an impact on my mental and physical health, and more importantly, has led to a breakdown in my marriage.

Here are six tips for developing a positive, healthy relationship with yourself:

1. Stop negative self-talk.

2. Do things that make you feel great, such as exercise or reading a book.

3. Do not work too much. You must, instead, try to find your real purpose in life, something we'll look at in a coming chapter. Remember, you are not your job.

4. Set positive goals that you can achieve.

5. Hang around kind, supportive people who never judge you.

6. Forgive yourself for your past mistakes and move onwards and upwards.

Cultivating a healthy relationship with yourself is a lifelong process–and it is the best investment you can ever make.

Spiritual Relationship

Many of us also have a relationship with God. Or, at least, we believe that there is something greater than ourselves out there. As I see it, this is essential for our well-being. Both religion and spirituality can have a positive impact on our mental health. They can both help us better tolerate stress because they help us find peace, purpose, and forgiveness—a safe place to be, mentally. However, benefits generally vary between the two, due to their difference in nature. Having a spiritual relationship may help you experience a sense of purpose or help you see something more to life.

I recommend praying and meditating to experience those benefits.

Indeed, relationships are vital to our survival and our happiness. One nice piece of advice that I love is the following from writer, Anne Lamont: "If you want to have loving feelings today, do loving things: be kind to people, especially the elderly and yourself."

Paying attention to others creates a kind of light-hearted high. Deepen a relationship. It may sound basic, but it can help deepen your sense of satisfaction and peace, and decrease your sense of loneliness.

Personal Network

Having a personal network is so important, and I'm talking about a network composed of real human beings that you meet with in person and that you talk to face-to-face. I've already talked about how virtual connections and social media don't work well to alleviate executive loneliness, so I won't go into that again. I simply want to emphasize that relationships with real humans, in the flesh, are crucial to emerging from, and staying out of, executive loneliness. Research shows that social connections are very important to our well-being. Having support from family and friends is important for our happiness and health, and that support is also vital to our ability to share information, learn from others, and seize economic and career opportunities.

I now want to take this discussion a bit further and argue that it isn't just any human connection that will offer you the connection you need to feel satisfied, happy, and challenged in a positive way. Even when I was in the depths of executive loneliness, I had plenty of time with others. We have to be selective in who it is we are surrounding ourselves with because, as we already know, it's common to adopt the behavior and mannerisms of the people we're surrounded with. I've seen it first hand in the seven different countries I've lived in. The first few days of living in a new country make a big impact on the rest of my experience in that country. Let me give you some examples.

When I moved to Vietnam, I lived in a hotel for my first month, and next to the hotel was a restaurant and a bar. After work one day early on, I walked into the bar and started a conversation with a few people and made lasting connections easily. They were regulars that frequented the bar more or less every day. And those people became my primary social circle. They were on a dart team, so I also joined the dart team. That was a part of my life for many years in Vietnam, and I'm still friends with them today. They influenced my life in Vietnam in a big way. And even though these are great people, our relationship revolved around the bar and drinking.

When I made the decision to move to Indonesia a few years later, I remembered my first experience in Vietnam, and I decided to take a different approach for Indonesia, even before moving there. I looked up some of the running clubs, swimming clubs, and also some of the cycling and triathlon clubs in Indonesia. I became a member of those clubs very quickly. In fact, the very first morning that I arrived in Indonesia, I met up with one guy and we went for a cycle ride together. That was the start of a long personal relationship.

We became very good friends. He was Indonesian, and he introduced me to the culture, and really our friendship just helped make my experience in Indonesia a positive one. I learnt some of the language in my new home, and on my last day there, I went for a bike ride with him. This is one example of how big a difference a personal network can make in your daily life.

So, in one country, my first social connections led me to have friends that I met in the bar. In another country, my personal network was made up of friends that I exercised with. That made a big difference to my lifestyle and well-being.

It doesn't matter if you're a child or an adult, because you will still be heavily influenced by what the people around you do. There's only so much we can decide for ourselves. And on the flip side, if you keep declining everyone's invites to places you don't want to go to, you'll be looked at as quite selfish. So, if you form the right relationships with the right people and build up healthy habits, it really does wonders.

An anonymous senior executive who is the founder, leader, and osteopath at a multidisciplinary health center acknowledged that talking with his oldest friends is central to keeping him grounded and out of executive loneliness. As he told me, "A small but very close group of friends outside of work is key, in my opinion, to mental wellness. They have no stake in what happens and allow me to be humorous. These are people, some I have known since I was four years of age, some are senior school friends, and some from university." To all readers, he emphasizes, "Stay in contact with old friends. Don't apologize for not speaking to them for ages. Start talking as if you chatted last week."

Caused-Based Groups

It is essential to accept our need for connection because the need for human connection is undeniable. I have found that the best way to feel connected to other people is to join a cause-based community group—an organization that stands for something that you value and care about. You will then be surrounded by like-minded peers whom you will connect with, value, and be able to be open with. In my case, I belong to a few of these organizations. Let me share them:

Samaritans of Singapore (SOS)—since I launched the fundraising campaign, Race to an End of Executive Loneliness, I have arranged keynote talks that I have delivered with the intention of raising awareness about this suicide prevention agency. I have also donated and raised funds for the organization, and will continue to service this community. I feel a strong connection with everyone involved with this project because we all strive for the same goal—to prevent suicides.

Support Group for Problem Drinkers—tthis group is anonymous, so I cannot share the name of it, but in this group, I have met other problem drinkers who faced a similar issue and problems like I had. We are now together on an amazing recovery journey, and while I have not consumed any alcohol for two-and-a-half years at the time of writing, others in this group have not had a drink for five, ten, or 20 years. We are not getting together to talk solely about drinking. We are getting together because we trust each other and can be honest and vulnerable with each other. We have real friendships, and we talk about our challenges in life and how to overcome them, but also about all the joy in life. We share our gratitude list with each other and help each other like we are a real family.

Running, Cycling, Swimming, and Triathlon Groups—II belong to several fitness and training groups, and I truly enjoy these groups. They offer a special kind of community, one that might lead to newfound exercise accountability as well as camaraderie. I've noticed that my relationships with people from these exercise groups are not as deep as the ones I have formed in community service and care groups, but they are still relationships with grounding and purpose. They are positive.

Before my crash into executive loneliness, I did not have the above beautiful and deep connections. I am today blessed for the mental health handicap that I experienced in my past, because it has opened up a whole new world to me. Join a cause-based community. Find an organization that supports a cause you care about, so you can surround yourself with those people.

We all need people to talk to. It can be friends, your husband or wife, a support group, a cycling club, a triathlon club, a running club, a knitting club, or whatever. The point is to make sure that your personal network is strategically built up and not randomly accumulated because, as the saying goes—"You are who you hang out with.."

Professional Network

It may sound like a cliché to say that it's lonely at the top, but in the case of senior executives, it appears to be true. A study carried out by *Harvard Business Review* found that half of the surveyed chief executive officers (CEOs) expressed feelings of loneliness, and 61 percent thought the issue hindered their performance at work. Psychologist Maria Micha pointed out that the driving reason executives experience loneliness is "when you are at the top, you are supposed to have all the answers. You are supposed to know everything."

Banking executive "Maureen", in the chapter *Be Vulnerable*, stated that those were the sentiments she felt and that contributed to her stress and isolation. That is, until Maureen got vulnerable and admitted to her team and bosses that she did not know everything and that she needed their support, she didn't feel any better.

Belonging to social groups is crucial for our mental health, and beyond that, we break free from isolating tendencies and connect with others through these networks.

Executive loneliness is particularly acute in Singapore, due to the lack of peers that senior executives have in the region. As executives grapple with an increasingly diverse set of challenges, ranging from rising protectionism to the threats and opportunities created by digitization, many find themselves with limited options on who they can turn to for advice. While CEOs and country directors in Europe typically have other people at their level in different countries across the continent whom they can consult for advice, a significant proportion of people at a high level in Asia are regional directors, meaning they do not have this option.

Executive loneliness in Singapore is further compounded by the fact that executives are often reporting to head offices in Europe or the US, meaning they have to work late to ensure there is an overlap in the two locations' working days. These long hours leave little time for developing a strong network, which could go some way towards alleviating feelings of isolation.

Ritu Mehrish, author and executive coach, observed, "Being part of a closely-knit networking organization is a very powerful avenue for executives to meet and share their challenges with like-minded people. There is immense power in collective thinking."

If the situation only impacted executives as individuals, it might be tempting to ignore it, but there is growing evidence that being part of an effective professional network has a significant positive impact on the businesses they head up, particularly if the business is in a growth phase or is expanding into new markets.

A Strong Professional Network

In his book *Connected Leadership*, Andy Lopata wrote that it is common for senior executives to neglect the importance of building and nurturing a professional network. There is simply not enough time. It seems like everything else is a priority and attending networking events seems to be a luxury. However, this is exactly the point of professional relationships: they are there to help you to get things done more quickly and with higher quality output. The network is there to guide and help you, you cannot know it all yourself and just looking internally in your company will not give you the innovative answers you're looking for. You need the diversity of an external professional network. You may also need the empathy that comes with it. Particularly in challenging times. It will be a source of inspiration and newfound energy and excitement, which will propel you to the next level. You will reach all of those deadlines more quickly and more efficiently.

Andy goes on to say that one of the biggest solutions to relieving stress, is being able to talk through a business challenge that is bothering you with another business person who has been there before. A mutual understanding will be quickly established with that trust, and the solution will be found in no time.

A professional network is important, especially for an executive, because you may be facing challenges in your business or in your work that you can't bring home to talk to your family about. You might feel frustrated that your husband or wife doesn't understand the challenges that you are faced with at work, but that frustration might be unfounded in that they likely won't be positioned to understand unless they work in the same industry.

It's often difficult to discuss these challenges within your organization, because the person you report to could be your boss, and perhaps they're based in another continent, and they've hired you as an expert for your country or market. When you discuss issues on Zoom or whatever conference call service you are using, your boss might think and say, "Why are you asking me about this? You're the expert. You're supposed to have all the answers. That's why we hired you." You end up thinking that they don't share the challenges you face, and you end up trying to show them what you can do, rather than what you can't.

For the same reason, you might not be able to discuss your challenges with people below you. Even if you're an area sales manager, you will have key account managers below you, reporting to you. They're the people you're supposed to be motivating and driving, so you might not have much leeway to share your challenges with them. And so, you end up not having many or any people to discuss work-related challenges with.

Many people are also fearful that colleagues they open up to will find a reason to stab them in the back to try and nab the next promotion from them. There are so many reasons why executives remain silent inside an organization and don't talk about their work, especially in regard to challenges. However, on the flip side, they'll be quick to celebrate their successes.

So, where can you take your professional challenges and where do you discuss them? You need a professional network, a safe place outside of your company you can rely on, and people you can network and be friends with. You can have a few friends that you trust and who trust you to speak honestly with. You can have a coach; many executives have a career coach. There are also a lot of networking opportunities where you can belong to a professional organization, for example, the Chamber of Commerce, the Women's Network, the Mentoring Men Network, and a wide array of confidential peer groups. As Andrew Bryant, executive and leadership coach and author, pointed out, "The right kind of network is important. A mastermind of people that you can trust and be yourself with is highly beneficial."

As mentioned earlier, I'm the co-founder and managing director of one such peer group, EGN (Executives' Global Network). We ask all members to sign a non-disclosure agreement so that what is discussed in these meetings is confidential. There's no way that it's going to leak out and find its way back to your company or your boss, if you discuss conflicts that are happening in your organization. You're looking for answers to those conflicts in your professional network, and you certainly don't want that to leak out.

We call it a "circle of trust" because you really should feel that you're in a trusted environment. I think it's better than just having one coach or mentor to ask for advice, because one person certainly doesn't have all the answers.

In such a professional network, you have 25 to 30 executives you can ask for advice. These networks have a facilitator who is certified to moderate the discussion and link expertise with the challenges. So there's a chance for you to test your challenges, test your ideas, and get input from various people. There will be some people there who have gone through that challenge before, so you don't have to go through the same pitfalls. I should add that the importance and power of a professional network is not built overnight. It's something you need to nurture over a long period of time.

Haider Manasawala, director and general manager of finance and planning at the Asia Pacific region of a big international company, has experienced firsthand the value of executive networks as a member of EGN Singapore. Haider said, "This is a good forum for exchanging thoughts and seeking reciprocal help in dealing with common challenges and opportunities. Its wide network of accomplished professionals acts as a valuable resource and a sounding board to bounce ideas off to gain fresh insights into problems and solutions that may not have been readily apparent." As Haider attested, despite their busy schedules, executives have shown time and time again their willingness to assist their peers. It does not need to be lonely at the top.

The senior executive whom we're calling "Boris" has also found EGN incredibly helpful in providing him support so that executive loneliness doesn't overrun him. Boris explained, "EGN has been a great help in terms of widening my horizons in terms of business, extending my network, and sharing ideas with others. It has been important."

Along the same lines, the senior executive we're calling "Seamus" reported: "I have developed both a formal and informal professional network. I joined EGN, which has been a great mechanism to engage with and share experiences, especially during COVID-19, but it has also meant that I have developed some good friendships with some of the EGN members whom I meet with regularly for coffee and to just chat about life and work experiences. I enjoy this as there is no judgement whatsoever. A professional network has also given me exposure to the latest thinking on a whole range of business and soft skills, which is a benefit that I did not expect. I also joined a less formal community group of fellow introverts, which has given me a social outlet in a comfortable and relaxed environment."

When it comes to executive loneliness, if you have this additional professional network, it's almost acting like your own personal and private advisory board. Say, for example, that you are feeling lonely and stressed because you don't have anyone to talk to about your challenges and when you come home, you also don't want to talk about this with your spouse. At that point, you have this network to reach out to, and as you're building this network over time, it includes face-to-face meetings, virtual meetings, and so on.

At EGN, as is common for many such professional networks, we have confidential chatrooms. We call it the Members of Universe, which is a mobile app where members can raise questions. So, no matter what question you're faced with—let's say you need to recruit new staff or you need to know about transfer pricing between Singapore and Vietnam—you can post it in the query section on the app. So, instead of having all these questions on your shoulders and walking around agonizing over them by yourself, you have a safe place where you can share and get level-headed responses.

Let me add too that something unique about EGN is the diversity of fields in our peer groups. Business leaders tend to have strong relationships within their own field, i.e., someone in the hotel industry will go to hospitality exhibitions and forums related to that field. But the magic really happens when people reach out to connect with people outside of their field. That is why, at EGN, we carefully look at the group DNA of each peer group, looking to find the most compelling match of 25 to 30 peers with various backgrounds. This fosters a culture of diversity, and more innovative ideas and solutions are found. To get a new, fresh take or a different take on the challenges you face is a breath of fresh air. The sooner we can accept that different industries share common problems, the faster we can get outside of our comfort zone and network with diverse people, and we will learn something new and we will grow ourselves and improve our business.

The point of EGN and other such professional support groups is that everyone faces challenges and issues at work. The only difference is that some decide to keep silent about it while others dare to be vulnerable and share their challenges inside the network of the peer group because that is where the power lies. And that is the solution to feeling much better and to escaping the trap of loneliness. And I would encourage people to do that.

Birds of a feather flock together–only executives can truly understand the stress of being at the top of the corporate ladder. With a support network of like-minded people, executives can receive dozens of answers to their burning questions.[1]

---

1. Source: https://sg.egn.com/insights/the-importance-of-peer-groups-to-executives

Professional Network, Retrenchment, and Recession

Those who've planned ahead and built a robust professional network are best prepared to weather a coming recession and face the specter of retrenchment. Even before the coronavirus crisis, uncertain conditions threatened numerous mid- to late-career executives. Transformative technology is rendering many formerly respected and highly paid jobs obsolete.[2] Globalization and the rationalization of roles have taken a heavy toll. Now, with an impending recession, companies are looking to reduce expenses wherever possible, simply in order to survive. The best-paid, most senior employees are frequently the first to be let go.

Few bounce back as quickly as they'd hope. In spite of their depth of experience and know-how, senior executives who are retrenched in middle age often struggle to re-enter the workplace. According to Singapore's Ministry of Manpower (MOM), in the third quarter of 2019, only 61 percent of professionals, managers, executives, and technicians (PMETs) found a new job within six months of being retrenched, versus 76.5 percent of clerical, sales, and services workers, and 72.8 percent of production and related workers. Those aged 40-plus stay unemployed longest. In the third quarter of 2019, 40 percent remained unemployed 6 months after being laid off.

Long-term unemployment results in great economic hardship and in the case of expats, many return to their home country, whether they like it or not—no matter how deep their roots in Asia. Many experienced executives are confident that, even if they are retrenched, they will quickly find a new job comparable in rank and pay-grade to their previous position through a recruiter or by applying for vacancies listed on LinkedIn and other sites. This is rarely the case. In my experience, 80 percent of senior executives find new roles through their professional networks.

To offer a salient example, I know one particular executive who, after being retrenched by a multinational company last year, applied for nearly 100 positions. All that effort came to nothing, despite this individual being in possession of a highly impressive resumé and decades of experience in his field. However, when he went out cycling with a friend, it turned out his companion knew of an appropriate position within his own company and could put in a resounding referral. He got the job.

---

2. Source: https://www.peoplemattersglobal.com/blog/life-at-work/could-networking-be-the-post-covid-19-career-lifesaver-25436

That's the power of a strong network. But a network isn't established overnight. People need to put in the time and effort to solidify their network before the dark clouds fill the sky. It's like physical fitness, you need to work on staying healthy and exercising while you're still in good physical condition. If you wait until your health starts to fail, it's too late.

As many will sadly discover as the coronavirus crisis plays out, those who think they have a job for life today are sadly mistaken. Yet still, a large number of top executives and leading professionals overestimate their employment security. Or they operate under the false impression that a new job will be easily found when needed, simply by contacting recruiters or trawling job listings. They are mistaken. It is invariably business contacts and relationships that create the connections leading to a new appointment.

The relationships leaders build with their peers are invaluable in allowing them to learn from one another, collaborate, share advice, overcome hardships, and thrive during periods of prosperity. But equally, the networks those executives forge prove literally lifesaving when they are faced with unemployment. Sending your resume to a recruiter is unlikely to result in a new job. Tapping a group of trusted associates in senior leadership roles, meanwhile, has proven over and over to be decisive in securing a new position.[3] In the upcoming chapter, Have a Plan B, I'll provide more information on my recommendations for efforts you can put in today to secure your future, should it be necessary.

If you feel it is time for you to expand your professional network and take action, reach out today and join a networking group near you. Should you happen to be based in Singapore, Malaysia, or Indonesia then you may want to fill in this form if you are interested in becoming a member: *https://www. egnsingapore.com/membership-form* or you can connect with or follow me on LinkedIn: *https://nickjonsson.com/linkedin.*

---

3.   Source: *https://sg.egn.com/insights/could-networking-be-the-post-covid-19-career-lifesaver*

Men vs. Women

Is it men or women who suffer the most from loneliness, depression, and mental illness? If you look at the statistics, it seems like men are suffering more from loneliness; it seems like women tend to have a few closer friends that they speak with. Many of my friends say their wife can talk for three hours on the phone with her friends, and keep talking away about anything and everything.

And men don't tend to do that as much. Men tend to view the world and have conversations in a more "efficient" way, which is not necessarily the best thing when it comes to deep and meaningful communication. Naturally, of course, that indicates that men feel a bit more lonely. But if we start to look into the statistics surrounding depression, it seems like women suffer more from depression in most countries. Why is that?

Perhaps it is because, if you are a woman, and you have a few close friends, and you tell them how you feel, a female friend will most likely encourage their friend to go see a doctor or therapist, or even take them there, while men tend to suffer in silence. So, I think underreporting plays a significant part in the discrepancy of the statistics. Here, the man is suffering by himself while the woman has already taken her first steps to recover from executive loneliness. She told her friend, and her friend has advised her to go see a doctor or therapist, while the man puts on a front and isn't diagnosed.

Another factor could be hormone imbalances, which cause moods to go up and down. And when we look at suicide attempts, we know that women attempt it more, which might be intended as a cry for help, while men attempt it less, but succeed more often. And perhaps it's because men are suffering in isolation that they resort to more extreme methods and more heavily commit to attempting suicide than women. They don't talk to anybody about it. There's no one around to recognize there is a problem, try to help them, or stop their attempt.

At least, that's my interpretation of the statistics, but clearly, both men and women are suffering.

About Female Executives

Additionally, especially if you are a woman working in a field that is heavily dominated by men, and you occupy a high position, it can be extremely isolating and lonely. In Singapore, it's only 12 per cent of board members that are women in high positions, so it's a man's world. It can be very challenging to get these women to open up, because they always need to be showing as much capability and dominance as they believe a man would in this position, and perhaps to a greater degree in order to earn the respect of their male subordinates. It can be a lonely affair for these reasons, and it's not surprising a lot of these female executives are under a lot of stress and have very few people to talk to in their position.

Make and Live Amends

No one is perfect. We are all humans, and we make mistakes throughout our lives. These stumbling blocks and errors help to mold us and build our characters through the experiences, both good and bad. There is no shame in admitting when we are wrong. Making amends is part of life, but it takes a strong and honest person to admit and correct their mistakes. We all leave some damaged or thorny relationships behind us. If we can identify them and make amends, we may feel just a bit less lonely and more connected and whole.

Making amends may seem difficult, but for those serious about recovering from executive loneliness, it can be fantastic for the spirit and the soul. Those making amends may find that the person they have harmed will often accept those amends happily—and each party may begin to heal as a result of this dialogue.

This is not always the case, however. Sometimes, the injured party is not willing to forgive and forget. If this is the case, don't dwell on it. The key is to keep your side of the street clean, so it does not matter if the other person forgives you or not. Making amends is a way to clean your side of the street, should you get it dirty.

What is an amend? An amend is not an apology. It is a purposeful act that involves confronting a past problem and helping both parties to move on from the situation.

If I caused harm or trouble for another person and want to make an amend, I would open a dialogue with that person, explain where I went wrong, accept my role in the situation, and say that I have and will continue to change as a person since the incident. If I owe them money or something material, I will make sure that I pay it back. The important part is taking responsibility.

Sometimes sitting down with someone isn't an option when making amends. In that case, send them a handwritten note or a postcard, or even an email.

Making amends does carry a condition—do not make amends with someone if doing so would open old wounds or create new ones. The potential benefit to one party does not outweigh the potential pain it may cause the other. Don't make amends if doing so would hurt others. Be righteously honest, but not ridiculously honest.

Taking Stock and Making Amends

Taking stock, as mentioned in an earlier chapter, and making amends go hand in hand. To review, taking stock is when you take an honest look at yourself and where you went wrong, and acted wrongly to others. This can go back a long way; it could be something you did or said to your colleague 20 years ago. It might be something you said or did to your brother 15 years ago; something that might have hurt him. It might be something you haven't really figured out yet. And you're walking around with all that baggage.

With taking stock, you compose a list of all the items that are bothering you. Once you've finished the list, you should really think about apologizing to the people you have hurt. It could be something that you just haven't cleared up yet. Once you've written everything down, think about taking action. This is where making amends comes in to play. When you take responsibility for your poor choices in the past and you make amends, you are able to free yourself from the weight of that stress and baggage. In turn, this lifts you from the abyss of executive loneliness. For this reason, it's very important to go back to those people you hurt and make it right. If possible, doing it in person is always best; perhaps meeting someone for lunch or coffee just to clear the air.

One of my own examples is something that happened to me in 2014, when my son was just five years old. In my sister's family, it was perfectly fine for children to have soft drinks with their meals. However, in my case, I was against my son drinking soft drinks. When my son saw that everyone else had a soft drink, my sister got him a soft drink too. And that was the first soft drink he had ever had in his whole life. This happened without anyone consulting me.

I remember being very upset about this. I made some rude comments, and I stormed off from this particular lunch. It was left undiscussed for many years, but it was still on my mind. The relationship with my sister wasn't destroyed entirely, but we didn't meet much afterward. Though it was a small incident, we didn't speak much at all for years. We live in different countries, and so we have different values. When we meet people with different values, it can easily result in misunderstandings that can lead to something bigger.

When I was taking stock, I made a huge list with similar incidents that bothered me. And I know personally that in walking around with all that baggage, it adds up quickly. If you have 100 bothersome incidents to do with relationships with your family and at work, it's very hard to move on. You can't get over your loneliness until you clear it up. I created a spreadsheet where I thought as far back as I could in my life, and wrote a list of all my insights that would help me make amends. I invited people to lunch or for a coffee, and if that didn't work, I would send them a postcard. In the worst case, I would send them a text or an email.

When I finally came around to making amends to my sister on a visit to Sweden two years ago, it seemed like she had already forgotten about that soft drink incident. And here I had been walking around with that pain inside for years. As soon as I made this amend to her, a sense of relief was lifted from my shoulders, and our relationship was healed. We even started to plan for a future holiday together.

When senior executive "Mario" was taking stock and looking to make amends, in this case with his colleagues regarding an incredibly stressful project and his own resulting executive loneliness, this is how he described the experience: "Since then, I've had discussions with over half of the team that were part of the troubled engagements and individuals who, in my view, didn't deliver—something I did make quite clear to some of them during that time. I met with them to restore the relation. Even if it remains clear I will not work with them again, at least we again can look each other in the eye. Two people, specifically, who were the initial governors of these engagements and responsible for their oversight up until the bubble burst, I had great difficulty forgiving and coming to terms with. With one, I sat down one day, perhaps a year after the facts, on a curb-side terrace, and we talked for easily two hours about the things that happened and we reconciled. The other I've only recently had a discussion with of a similar nature, after having avoided him for several years—I would not have been able to have a meaningful discussion with him anyway, until I had given things a place for myself. The discussion was strange and uncomfortable—something exacerbated by the fact he works for a competitor now—and in the end I think we've come to terms with one another's involvement and views."

Living Amends

When you talk about things like this, especially things that happened in your family or at work, after clearing it up, it's something that is lifted from your shoulders. We're clearing away the old garbage and moving on to the next stage, which is living amends. Living amends means to apologize on a daily basis; it means to catch yourself every day when you don't act your best and apologize for it. That way, if you do something wrong, or you say something rude—which is easy when you're very busy, and something pops up, and you say something you don't mean—you apologize for it. Why bother hurting yourself and creating new baggage that you'll walk around with for years? It's better just to apologize as soon as you recognize that you've done something wrong.

In the evening, you can think about what you did during the day and whether there was something that wasn't cleared up. Did you say something that caused a misunderstanding with a colleague or a family member? Try to clear it up by the end of the day or the next day. If you can, you can just pick up the phone and call the person or send them a message saying, "Sorry, I didn't really mean that," just to clear it up. Before you go to bed every night, take stock. It's amazing.

Something I learnt in my support group is that when you're dealing with addicts who might be prone to relapsing, one of the biggest causes is tension. It builds up over time and then triggers that person when they're not feeling great, to pick up drugs or alcohol again. And it doesn't apply only to these traditional vices; you can slip back into old bad habits that will push you back into loneliness and depression easily. You can reduce tension by taking stock of your behavior and making amends when necessary. This is a way to emerge from and stay out of the negative space of executive loneliness.

Trying to clear up misunderstandings and apologize for things you said or did on the spot, or soon after, makes you feel so much better. You won't be walking around obsessing about what you've done wrong in the past. It's such a great relief. And in terms of loneliness, it will make you feel much more connected to others, knowing that there's no one in the world that you've stopped being honest with.

If somebody else says or does something unkind, and you are tempted to carry that around, you need to ignore it and move on with your life. The most you can do is keep your side of the street clean. That's all you can do. There will always be someone who will say or do something that's not nice, but just like on social media, if you read something that really upsets you, you can either pick a fight with them, or you can just ignore it. And nothing will happen. It's the same with everything in life.

You will find that there are family members or colleagues that say or do something that bothers you. Maybe they haven't developed a habit of coming back to apologize, and they just leave it like that. But the key message is that when you feel great, ignore the rest.

To most of us, making amends will take the rest of our lives, but we can start immediately. It is a part of our process of becoming a better person.

I would like to challenge you to take a sheet of paper and write down three people who you can make amends with right away. You might have many more people in mind, but start with three to get this positive cycle in motion.

Chapter Summary—Healthy Relationships

Establishing robust relationships with friends, family members, colleagues, and other executives is key in helping you find your way out of executive loneliness and in helping you stay out of it once you emerge. We looked at the critical issue of fostering healthy relationships in order to emerge from and stay out of executive loneliness in the following five ways:

One: The Importance of Healthy Relationships

All people, even top executives, need to establish healthy relationships to create bonds, friendships, and provide needed emotional support. Relationships are an effective way of helping someone who is suffering mentally to recover. Relationships are also key to helping a person avoid falling into the loneliness trap. With good relationships, we feel better, and the stronger the relationship, the better we can show up. It is a safe space where we can be ourselves without fear. Accordingly, healthy and robust relationships are critical to getting out, and staying out, of executive loneliness.

Two: Personal Network

RResearch shows that social connections are very important for our well-being. Having support from family and friends is important for our happiness and health, and that support is also vital to our ability to share information, learn from others, and seize economic and career opportunities. Even still, we have to be selective in who it is we include in our personal network because, as we already know, it's common to adopt the behavior and mannerisms of the people we're surrounded with. Seek out positive, supportive individuals, as well as inspiring and fun cause-based groups to establish a strong and fulfilling personal network.

Three: Professional Network

The point of having a professional network is for there to be other professionals who are there to help you get things done more quickly and with higher quality output. The network is there to guide and help you, as you cannot know it all yourself and simply looking within your company will not give you the innovative answers you need. You need the diversity of an external professional network. You may also need the empathy that comes with it. Particularly in challenging times. It will be a source for inspiration and newfound energy and excitement, which will propel you to the next level. You will reach all those deadlines more quickly and more efficiently. All of this, in turn, allows you to experience less stress and anxiety, which keeps you far away from executive loneliness.

Four: Men vs. Women

Though men and women may experience and address executive loneliness differently, it is something anyone can experience, whether you're male or female, so prepare for it. Engage in the steps, as well as further recommendations given in this book, to help you build a strong foundation for keeping executive loneliness at bay.

Five: Make and Live Amends.

We all leave some damaged or thorny relationships behind us. If we can identify them and make amends, we may feel just a bit less lonely and, instead, more connected and whole. Living amends means to apologize on a daily basis; it means to catch yourself every day when you don't act your best and apologize for it. Trying to clear up misunderstandings and apologize for things you wrongly said or did on the spot, or soon after, makes you feel so much better. You won't be walking around obsessing about what you've done wrong in the past when you make and live amends. It's such a great relief. And in terms of loneliness, it will make you feel much more connected to others, knowing that there's no one in the world that you've stopped being honest with.

Create Goals and Write a Gratitude List

I learnt from reading the books of Brian Tracy, the importance of writing goals and how that encourages us to live and be our best. According to Brian Tracy, we must all have a major definite purpose for our life. We must have one goal that, if we accomplish it, can do more to help us improve our life than any other single goal. Here are three powerful quotes from Brian Tracy around goals:

- "It doesn't matter where you are coming from. All that matters is where you are going."

- "All successful people are big dreamers. They imagine what their future could be, ideal in every respect, and then they work every day toward their distant vision, that goal or purpose."

- "People with clear, written goals accomplish far more in a shorter period of time, than people without them could ever imagine."

In 2010, along with the Canadian Chamber of Commerce Vietnam and ITD World, I had the pleasure of sponsoring Brian Tracy to come to Vietnam. I attended this full-day event with my staff and key customers, and had the pleasure of personally meeting Brian, a lovable man that we can learn so much from. It was life-changing. I made a promise to Brian and myself to always write my goals in the simple way that he taught me.

Setting goals is also an important step in the recovery from mental illness and in emerging from or avoiding executive loneliness. Let me explain how this has worked for me. The times of my life when I have been well enough to remember to spend five minutes each morning to write down my goals, I have always felt better. It is the times when I start forgetting to write goals that, step-by-step, I fall away from achieving great things, and with this, my mood also slowly decreases. Today, I can look back and read my goals as far back as 2010, and what is amazing is to see that most of my bigger achievements have been captured there. It seems like everything in my life has happened twice, first in my mind and in my goal writing, and then in reality.

When I have been off the beam and not performing at my best, and when I had mental challenges, I can see that I was not writing any goals during those times. It seems like I, therefore, did not have a clear focus and was just drifting around during the time periods when I wasn't writing goals. I should have remembered that Brian told us, "If what you are doing is not moving you towards your goals, then it's moving you away from your goals." I wish I would have reminded myself during those times to spend five minutes writing my goals down to get back on track. I cannot imagine a large, successful company or a football team that did not have a strategy or clear goals and targets, so how can we as individuals possibly run our own lives in a successful manner without written goals? It's like driving around in the fog, and if we press on and work harder, it is like turning on the car's high beams when driving in fog, meaning, our lack of direction and inability to see gets even worse! We must write our goals to get crystal clear about what we want to achieve if we are to make progress in our lives.

Andrew Bryant, an executive and leadership coach, and the author of *Self Leadership: How to Become a More Successful, Efficient and Effective Leader* from the Inside Out knows a lot about the relationship between setting goals and emerging from executive loneliness. Andrew explained it like this: "Goal-setting focuses the individual on a future self. Working with an executive coach will facilitate who a person wants to become, what they want to do, and what they want to have. Once an executive has become self-aware of their patterns of loneliness, setting goals focuses them on becoming a person who is connected and purposeful. They will work with the coach to know exactly what to do, and be clear about the results they want to have."

Author and executive coach Ritu Mehrish observed, "People going through executive loneliness experience a lack of clarity and objectivity. They need to step back and ask themselves, 'What is it that I want and how is my current situation stopping me from getting there? Am I doing anything that is hampering the big goal? What do I need to do to get closer to my goal?' It is difficult to do this on our own as it's tough, if not impossible, to be completely objective and honest with ourselves. We need someone to probe us, nudge us, provoke us, and challenge us to think deeper and come up with answers. The best person to do that is an executive coach!"

A Variety of SMART Goals

Here are the goals that I wrote for myself today:

1. My *Executive Loneliness* book has been released globally on Amazon by Month, Day, Year, and is a best-seller by Month, Day, Year.

2. I have received at least ten positive reviews of my book on Amazon by Month, Day, Year.

3. I have completed Ironman (triathlon) Kalmar Sweden in less than 12 hours and 25 minutes by Month, Day, Year.

4. I have $45,000 in savings as an emergency fund in my bank account by Month, Day, Year.

5. I weigh 77 kilograms by Month, Day, Year.

6. My company, EGN Singapore has 500 members by Month, Day, Year.

7. EGN has successfully launched EGN Malaysia by Month, Day, Year.

8. I have seen my son who lives in Sweden, while I live in Singapore, at least twice yearly.

9. My wife and I have a baby by Month, Day, Year.

10. My medical check results will be good (I keep measurable targets for each value such as cholesterol, blood pressure, etc.) by Month, Day, Year.

In just five minutes, I wrote the above goals. What I've found is that if you write your goals daily, some more and/or new things will pop up each time, e.g., goals around finances, charity activities, life purpose, etc. The key is not to overthink this, just get started.

As you can see from my brief list of goals, the goals touch on a variety of areas in my life.

Purpose: I have a goal that includes success with this book, which is important and leads to my purpose in life: to help others and to reduce the stigma surrounding mental health.

Health and fitness: There is also a goal around health and fitness with a triathlon, which will remind me to eat healthy and exercise daily. I even put a weight goal there because I will remind myself to weigh myself each morning to be on track.

Business: I put in business goals in regards to my company EGN where I am the co-founder and managing director.

Family relationships and connection: There are goals related to spending time with my son, as to making living amends for the lack of time I did not spend with him when I was sick. There is also a goal to have a baby with my wife, because I know how much this means to her.

Health and fitness (again): I have a medical test goal to remind myself to go to the doctorand check how I am doing. I also want to capture anything happening internally, that I cannot feel, to prevent something serious from popping up.

There could be many new goals, such as learning a new hobby, walking five kilometers daily, cycling three times a week, taking singing lessons, showing up to my support group four times per week, and learning the French language.

The point is to show you that it is important to have goals for multiple areas of your life. At ICF coaching, we look at the "wheel of life", which looks at the parts of an individual's life: career, finance, personal growth, health, family, relationships, social life, and attitude. To use the wheel of life, you look at each part of your life and rate yourself in that area from 1-10, where a 10 reflects exactly how it should be for you, and 1 reflects that the reality is as far away as it could be from your ideal. You can then set goals for all those areas to improve and strive for a 10, in all parts of your life. It is essential to create balanced and well-rounded goals.

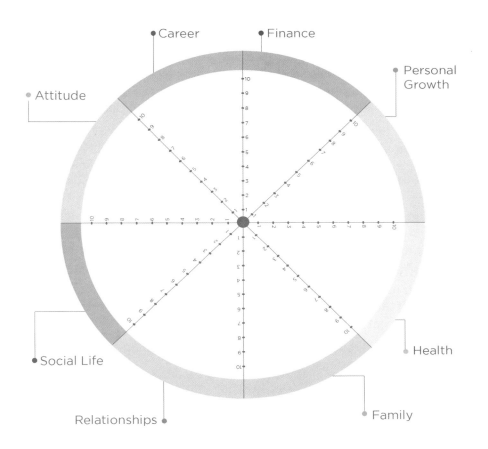

Notice, too, that my goals follow the SMART goal system. This means they are specific, measurable, achievable, realistic, and anchored within a timeframe. Using the SMART goal-setting criteria for making your goals will better help you to reach success. If you aren't familiar with SMART goals, then you can easily look it up by doing an internet search to learn more about this valuable tool.

Once you've made your goals, then you determine the small steps you must take to reach and achieve each goal. By setting ourselves a series of mini-goals that lead to us reaching a bigger goal, we are able to make the bigger goal more manageable and reachable. This is how, in 2013, I crossed my first-ever marathon finish line well within my target of four hours (I did it in three hours 53 minutes). I had, over three years' time, learnt to run, starting from three kilometers, to five kilometers, ten kilometers, and now 21 kilometers, and I have slowly stretched the goals over these years. Start by taking small steps towards your goal. Remind yourself that the best way to eat an elephant is one bite at a time.

But what are we supposed to do when our ultimate goal has been achieved? My answer: there is always something higher or different to aim for. Let it fall off your goal list, and something else will take its place. Just make sure to have your overarching purpose goal crystal clear.

If you do this goal-setting exercise with a coach, they may help you to do mind mapping, so your goals can be aligned to the wheel of life. A mind map represents ideas and concepts visually. It helps structure information and helps you to better analyze and generate new ideas. Just as with every great idea, the power of a mind map lies in its simplicity. If you'd like to learn more about mind mapping, there is a great book on this topic written by Tony Buzan called *The Mind Map Book: How to Use Radiant Thinking to Maximize Your Brain's Untapped Potential.*

Check out this saying by Norman Vincent Peale: "Shoot for the moon. Even if you miss, you'll land among the stars." Apply this to goals and set goals so that they make you dream big. That way, even if you miss them, you still achieve great results.

Fall into this habit. Set goals. Achieve them. Set bigger goals. Achieve them too. Repeat. And never give up!

Gratitude

Just as regularly recording your goals will help you aim big and stay out of executive loneliness, regularly recording what you are grateful for in your life helps you the same way. Plus, writing a gratitude list is fun and simple. Just write down the things that you are grateful for, whether it be people, places, animals, feelings, things, activities, memories, sounds, tastes, or the weather. Anything and everything that you are grateful for. Making a gratitude list helps us to recognize these blessings and keep our focus on the good things in our lives, as opposed to dwelling on our worries or past challenges. This is especially helpful when times get a little tough. Keeping a gratitude journal and writing daily gratitude lists is extremely beneficial during recovery, or to get out of executive loneliness, because it guides you to focus on the positive.

The aim of a gratitude list is to help people focus on the good things in their life. People tend to dwell on the bad and undervalue the good things, but journaling allows you to do the opposite and focus on your blessings. Keep a record of everything you're grateful for and you'll find that it's easier to maintain a positive attitude in daily life.

Some of the benefits of journaling whilst recovering from executive loneliness include:

- A gratitude list will help prevent you from forgetting how much progress you've made in recovery and help motivate you to keep moving forward.
- Regularly dwelling on the good things in life helps you maintain a positive outlook.
- You are less likely to relapse or undermine your progress if you remain grateful for what you have now.
- When you're feeling down, you can read your gratitude list and remind yourself of what you have to be grateful.
- Journaling can help you more accurately chart your progress in emerging from executive loneliness.

In my support group, we are encouraged to send our daily gratitude list to each other. It is a simple and wonderful habit that also encourages accountability to this positive practice. And it offers a positive start to each day. You can send this list daily as a message to your close friends. See their response! To inspire you, I'll share the list of things I'm grateful for as of today:

- My son's health
- My health
- My wife
- Clean water I drink
- My apartment
- My morning walk
- My upcoming trip to Sweden
- That I never have to be hungry
- My new computer
- That I am writing this book
- My upcoming keynote talks
- That I have so many great friends
- My recent coach certification

Now it's your turn. Pause and go to a notebook, piece of paper, or your computer or phone, and record ten things you are grateful for right now.

Create Goals and Write a Gratitude List | 187

Send it to a friend and start a gratitude exchange today.

Going Public

You can work with your coach to set some achievable goals and have your coach hold you accountable, or like Brian Tracy, you can develop them yourself and share them on social media. You see, once you put your goals out in public, you are more motivated to pursue them. For example, I shared my goal of writing this book on Facebook. And it's true. Putting it out there to my friends, family, and colleagues has held me accountable at a high level. Different methods work better for different people, so decide which method you want to use to help hold yourself accountable.

After you've set goals, track them. For health and fitness goals, there are great tools for tracking your progress and reaching your goals; tools like the Garmin watch, the Strava app, and MyFitness Pal. Use these digital tools to track what you eat, how much you're sleeping, and how much exercise you're doing. Finally, when you do those things, expect the best.

We end this chapter with another challenge. Your challenge is to write down ten goals for yourself or ten things you are grateful for and send them to a friend.

Find Your Passion-Hobby

Let's talk about your passions and your hobbies, because spending time doing activities outside of work that you most enjoy, can improve your mental health and well-being. Engaging with your passions and your hobbies can lift you out from, and keep you out of, executive loneliness. Research shows that people with hobbies are less likely to suffer from stress, low mood, and depression. Activities that get you out and about, both active and socializing, can leave you feeling happier and more relaxed.1

When I asked a friend of mine, global nomad, executive coach, and TEDx speaker Kevin Cottam, to explain how finding one's passion can help a person overcome executive loneliness, he first explained the trap of loneliness: "Loneliness is not the same as being alone; it is mentally made. It is your mind that tells you that you are 'alone', that creates negative, narrow messages and finds 'proof' you are lonely. This narrowing of your mindset reduces your ability to make choices and to see opportunities and possibilities. This then drives you down a narrow passageway, leading potentially to what appears as little hope. This reduces your energy, and your energy is what drives your whole being and the way you step into the world."

To explain how a passion can release you from this trap, Kevin pointed out: "Finding what you are passionate about starts to expand your mindset and thinking patterns by focusing on what it is that you really love. This increases your energy. It can be the simplest of things–such as listening to music, playing a sport you loved and have left behind, having great conversations, smiling at someone, meditating, and making others feel loved and wanted. The list can go on. Your core self knows what it is that you love, but you may have put it in a box with a padlock and thrown away the key. Finding your passion is like putting the key in the door, opening the

---

1. *Source: https://consciouscontent.org/connection-between-hobbies-and-mental-health/*

door, and walking through it boldly. It will expand your mind. Everyone is passionate about something; we just rarely take the time to look for it, as we are running on automatic."

To determine what you are passionate about, you must consider what you genuinely love to do and how you genuinely love to feel the emotion that comes up spontaneously, when you're doing what you love. It must come from you. Having a passion for something not only builds your confidence but also your resilience, which ultimately helps your mental health. It then provides stress relief, improves self-esteem, and builds your ability to fight against loneliness. With the long working hours required by executives these days, it is essential to have a passion outside the office. It is key to mental health. Or as Criss Jami said: "Prioritize your passion. It keeps you sane."

Some hobbies have been proven to reduce stress. For example, listening to music. Listening to music for at least a half-hour each day can lower your blood pressure, slow your heart rate, and calm anxiety and stress, according to Harvard Health Publishing. Other stress-reducing hobbies include dancing, shopping, walking, and watching movies.

Social connections are an important part of whatever hobby you choose when you're recovering from loneliness and depression. At the very least, you need to put effort into choosing a healthy hobby that enriches your life. Having a hobby that takes you out of your headspace at work is essential.

"Wrong" vs. "Right" Hobbies

Having a hobby makes a huge difference to your life. When it's the "wrong" hobby, you better believe it makes a huge difference. And the same is true when it is the "right" hobby for you, with that huge difference being in the positive direction. This is something I can attest to from firsthand experience, having picked up the wrong hobby after moving to a new country. I've touched upon my experience in Vietnam in an earlier chapter, when I explained how I made friends with people at the pub and joined the darts team, and how a lot of my life there revolved around drinking, which ultimately didn't have a positive effect on my life. After moving to Indonesia, I was proactive in finding the "right" hobbies. I joined a running club, a swimming club, and a cycling club. The people there became my friends, and I really started focusing on nurturing those healthy habits and hobbies.

When things get tough at the workplace, which they naturally do at times, it's great to have a healthy hobby to immerse yourself in outside of that headspace. It's also good to have some strong personal relationships that you have forged through those hobbies where you can have honest conversations. It's very important to have a hobby where you meet people in person, without relying so much on social media, where so many misunderstandings can occur so easily.

The Powerful Lift a Hobby Provides

Having a hobby has significantly helped me better my life, and it played a huge part in my recovery. I now cycle four to five times a week, and I've done so since I started my recovery in 2018. I've found life more challenging during lockdown, but because of these strong healthy habits that I have made a persistent part of my life, it's easier. Even if I have to cycle by myself. Recently, we've been allowed to cycle together with other people in smaller groups, which means I can enjoy my hobby (exercise) and talk to people (make and maintain connections).

Whenever I feel stressed or fatigued from being overworked, I now know what I need to do. I need to block some time off for myself, do something I love to do, and go cycling. For me, it only takes a basic bike ride in a single morning, and I feel instantly better. It shifts my mood completely and sets me nicely up for a positive and happy day. I can easily deal with the challenges that the day brings when I have my morning bike ride. I also try to combine my bike ride with socializing, either professional networking or with some of my friends from the support group.

Think about the hobby you are passionate about and keep that close to your heart, to pull out your sleeve if you ever feel stressed or on your way to burnout. I even ask my wife to remind me to go out for a bike ride if she sees I am tense. Sometimes we may not catch ourselves, so it is great to have someone reminding us.

Enjoying & Connecting, Not Achieving

Too many people—including me, until just two years ago—define ourselves by the work we do every day, even if we aren't passionate about it. I made that mistake when I started in university. I prided myself on studying extremely hard, getting the top score in as many classes as possible, and earning a scholarship. And when you put so much pressure on yourself to always deliver, you start to define yourself by your success. Some might say that this is a great habit, but I didn't change this attitude when I started working and it became a big problem. I'll explain what I mean.

When you're working with many people, and you're constantly pushing yourself to achieve, it will lead to difficult relationships because you're always trying to perform the best, meaning you get competitive. When I first started working, I did some group work, but a lot of what I did was my own deliverables. That's not a great habit to have when working in a company, because you should be doing your best to work as a team. It should be about helping the team grow, rather than being competitive to make sure you personally stand out. As I see it, this applies to all passions and interests a person might have. In order for them to provide connection, joy, and stress relief, your attitude can't be about competition and achievement. That's stress-inducing. Your mindset needs to be one that, first and foremost, is looking to enjoy the camaraderie and experience, and hopefully, but perhaps not, some results will follow.

Avi Liran, "chief delighting officer", delightful leadership and positive culture transformation expert, coach, mentor, and TEDx Speaker at delivering delight, explains the value of enjoying and connecting really well. Here's what Avi said: "I found my passion very early in my life. I had a desire since I was young to be a contributor to a happier world. I found that when people are smiling and laughing, it makes my day." For Avi, it was life's great tragedies that taught him the importance of joy, connection, and delight: "The struggle of my parents to survive the Holocaust, and then make it their life's mission to serve others, acted as my foundation."

"When my father passed away, I was 12 years old. It gave me perspective about life." Avi said about life's difficult times: "[They] taught me a lesson that I need to have more compassion to people who fall into that trap [i.e., depression]. I was not invincible anymore, and that made me more authentic, relatable, and helpful. It made me realize that I can only help people by being on their same level, feeling their pain, but not dwelling in it. Offering them a pathway to their delightful self, so they can climb up on my hands to start the journey beyond recovery, towards flourishing."

Here are Kevin Cottam's recommendations for how to figure out your passions and hobbies:

1. Go to a place, outside or inside, that you find boosts your energy. Bring a notepad or journal.

2. Observe what surrounds you externally and start to feel that inside– as part of you.

3. Be still and alert, listen, and observe. Then breathe and ask yourself, "What activities or things do I love to do? How do I love to be?"

4. Then capture that in two columns, "Do" and "Be", in your journal. Don't stop until you have 100 total in both columns.

5. The secret then is to start by taking one such item that you have recorded and start living it. This is a passion, it is your new friend, and it will drive your energy upwards. You start with one item and add in more and more to fill your life with joy.

Don't Put It Off

AAlexander Mearns has vast experience in working with executives to conquer executive loneliness. A common roadblock among his executive clients that hinders them from pursuing their passions and hobbies, is that they don't make them a priority. As Alexander explained it, "So many people we come across say, 'Oh, well, you know, I'd love to do this and that, but I'm just too busy at the moment'. That's a classic excuse, and it's really a big problem because you're always going to be busy if you have that attitude and you're never going to have enough time. With that kind of attitude, know that work can always be an excuse. You actually need to put all of that on hold and focus on the things that you need to do that are important in your life for getting healthy and fit, physically and mentally. Cancer, heart disease—they're not going to wait around until you're not busy. It's just going to come up and hit you on the head."

The takeaway is don't put off doing the things that bring you happiness. Don't give excuses. Set aside the to-do list and enjoy the people and activities that bring you happiness every day.

In closing this chapter, I challenge you to enact the five steps from Kevin Cottam, make that list, and then get started. Start living your passion and take notice of how that positively affects your feelings of loneliness.

Find Your Purpose

A recent speaker at an EGN event in Singapore named Mac McKenzie, co-founder of the Bridge Institute, said, "We define personal purpose as the intersection of talent–the capacities and powers that come naturally to you; passions–what you love to do and makes you come alive; and societal need–what the world really needs of you. When a person discovers their purpose in life, they flourish as human beings. They become psychologically and physically happier. They become a beacon of hope and a magnet for others. Finding your purpose in life is, perhaps, one of the best antidotes to executive loneliness."

Andrew Bryant, executive and leadership coach and author, observed: "Loneliness is spiraling inward. Having a purpose focuses the mind outwards. Having a purpose that involves other people expands experience and helps the executive to break the spiral of loneliness."

Kevin Cottam said this about living with purpose: "When you have and act with purpose, it makes your life much easier, because when you are walking into conversations, making choices, and leading yourself and others, it comes from a place much bigger than you. It has more air, it is freer, you can be much more productive, and your performance skyrockets with ease. Having a purpose is like being the 'megaphone': the narrow part is your inner voice and the wide part is your voice bellowing out and acting upon what you are authentically giving to the world. When you have a purpose, loneliness disappears because your life has more reason for being."

Ritu Mehrish, author and executive coach, noted that after the person in the executive position has achieved the financial, social, and status goals they've been chasing, then they will find themselves in need of a deeper meaning. Ritu argues that having a purpose provides the executive the "compass of life" they most need: "Having a clearly defined purpose helps leaders stay on track, stay focused and grounded. It helps us to look at life more holistically. Our work is one part of our life, but what about satisfaction, happiness, and contribution? Once we have defined our purpose, it becomes easier to put things in perspective and take action accordingly. Purpose is like the GPS that helps us find the correct route and also shows us how to locate new paths if one is blocked."

Ritu goes on to recommend to executives looking to stay out of executive loneliness: "Revisit and realign to your purpose. Step back and get a bigger perspective. Ask yourself, 'Are my actions and thoughts aligned to my purpose?' Figure out when the last time you tweaked your purpose or realigned yourself to it was."

This resonates with me since I came to life after my friend's suicide. I knew I had to do something. I knew I had to do everything I possibly could to help others from not falling into this trap. Giving back to my family, friends, and community will now be with me for life. Thus, being of service became my life purpose.

Finding Purpose and Looking to Something Greater

My support group meetings have also helped me to discover the importance of having an overarching life purpose that reflects what I value and that provides my life with meaning. When attending the meetings, I was encouraged to look for something greater than myself in this world. That's something that scares many people away from entering this journey. We live in a world where fewer and fewer people believe in the existence of a God. A lot of people are turned off from joining some support groups if they think a group could be a religious sect. It scares people away as soon as the word "God" is mentioned.

However, with the support group program I'm involved in, I learnt that it is very important to look for something greater than yourself in the universe, because if you think you are the center of the universe and nothing can be bigger than you, then it is very hard to come out of yourself and be humble in your loneliness and then to recover. If you really are the center of your universe, you are not open to change. That is what the support group program is about. This resonated with me, and I could accept this.

I am not sure what kind of God I believed in when I joined the support group, at least I could not picture the God or put a name to it. The good thing was that I did not have to explore this. I just needed to start to believe in a power greater than myself. Just by doing this, things started to open up for me, and I became more open-minded. I started to question my existence and think about my purpose in life. Is it just working hard, making money, collecting accolades and achievements, and every other material thing in life? Or was I here to do something more?

As I continued my recovery journey, and I read more and opened my mind further, I came to the conclusion that yes, there is something bigger than myself. I started searching for my own purpose and thought for a long time about what I could do. And it was through this process that I gained further affirmation that "being of service" is my life's purpose.

One of the female executives I interviewed for this book had a similar experience in terms of connecting to a higher spiritual force to help her stay out of executive loneliness. This is how she explained it: "I can't say that I have fully emerged from executive loneliness, but I can say that I am aware, I am fully committed, and I am involved to find the best that I have to offer, while being transparent and sincere to anyone who interacts with me. I know my purpose and I feel strongly towards it each day because I feel time is running out to do something about my passion and purpose. I don't let my profession define me anymore, and I don't let my work be the priority, because I work for other priorities in life. I am also spiritually connected to a greater sense of belonging in this universe with purpose, and that keeps me motivated too."

Grant's Purpose-Driven Life

Grant "Axe" Rawlinson, human-powered explorer and team decision-making coach at Powerful Humans, Pte Ltd, told me the following story around his personal quest for purpose and what it's like to finally live his life with a central purpose:

It took me many years, in fact not until I was around 40 years old, to understand that my life purpose was human-powered exploration. This realization came as an enormous relief to me. In hindsight, it had been staring me in the face for many years.

For much of my life, I had struggled with feelings of confusion around what made me truly happy versus what I should be doing. I began working in the corporate world, sitting in meetings, flying around the world, a steady salary, good career prospects, a great company. I remember thinking, "Surely this is what life should be about? Surely I should be happy?" But every morning when I woke up and looked in the mirror as I brushed my teeth, I knew something wasn't right. I yearned to be outdoors, in my boat, crossing a sea, cycling across a continent, or climbing a mountain in some remote part of the world.

In my twenties, when all of my friends were only interested in going to nightclubs, I would set off on long walks by myself. I couldn't find anyone to walk with me for the amounts of time I would be away, so I would generally go solo. But doing things alone was not cool at all, especially in the social circles

I came from. I still remember how embarrassed I would feel telling my friends my plans. One evening, one of them even called me a "loser" in front of a large group.

However, once I came to understand that human-powered exploration was more than a weird hobby, and that it was fundamentally what my life purpose was, my life changed. I no longer cared what people felt or thought about my expeditions and doing things alone. I quit my job and started my own business using the themes of my human-powered journeys to teach teams and leaders how to make more effective decisions. I stopped fighting my instincts and brought the different areas of my life closer together and more aligned around this purpose of human-powered exploration.

I am happier now than I have ever been; however, it is still lonely at times. Especially hard is not so much being away in my boat at sea by myself for months on end, but the planning and preparation for major expeditions. This takes years and often I am the only one who truly believes or cares in the project. It can be depressing at times, facing setback after setback with no one to support you. However, instead of feeling embarrassed about my journeys, I now understand it's my purpose and that gives me enormous strength.

I feel incredibly lucky that I am able to lead a purpose-driven life as opposed to my old life, which now seems hollow and empty. And even though my life is perhaps lonelier now than it was when I was surrounded by corporate colleagues, it is much more fulfilling.

Unsure of Your Purpose?

If you aren't sure of your purpose, Avi Liran, "chief delighting officer", gives the following recommendations to help you locate it: "When I was depressed, I resented people giving me cliched advice like, 'You can't really love others if you do not love yourself'. The idiot that formed this sentence probably never experienced hardship or has very little empathy. When I was depressed, I did not know how to love myself. What I needed were steps to get there. And I could love others. I could love my family and friends. So it is BS. When depressed, giving love is being around love, even if you are hurting inside. Doing something good for others is purposeful. Studies confirm that being generous with others and contributing to those less fortunate, even if it is just giving your time, is the seventh best thing that you can do for your own mental and physical health. If you are unsure of your purpose or your passion, giving to others is what you could do to transform from helpless to helpful."

Here's how Kevin Cottam recommends finding your purpose: "To find and live on purpose, you have to want it so badly. In many ways, it could be one of your passions. To uncover your purpose, you need to get curious and go 'nomad-ding' inside of yourself, deeply observe the world, and come back to the question, 'What is important to me?' I invite you not to stop until you find it. Just remember, life is a journey to find your purpose, and it can take a long time as you try life out and act: fail, succeed, fail, succeed. This gives you more reason for what is important. Your purpose counts; it will give you such incredibly energy to act, give, and be."

Part of our journey is to find our life purpose. In my case, it is about giving back to my family and friends and carrying out community service and to do what I could not do when I was sick. My life purpose is to be of service for the rest of my life, one day at a time. Now it is your turn: what is your life purpose?

Be of Service

Brian Tracy once said, "Successful people are always looking for opportunities to help others. Unsuccessful people are always asking, 'What's in it for me?'" As you know from previous chapters, I greatly esteem Brian Tracy and I'm a devotee to being of service, so you'd better believe I consider those words from him to be gold standard!

In the chapter before this one, I shared that my life purpose is to be of service to others. In that chapter, Avi Liran also recommended to anyone not sure of their life purpose, that they can find it if they start by being of service, or as he said it, "Giving to others is what you could do to transform from helpless to helpful."

Being of service, volunteering your time, work, money, etc., also provides many benefits to both your mental and physical health. Volunteering helps counteract the effects of stress, anger, and anxiety. Volunteering combats depression. It makes you happy. It increases your self-confidence. And, as already mentioned, volunteering provides you with a sense of purpose. When you volunteer, you're with other people who share similar values, so there's often an instant connection. Be giving. The person in need will feel gratitude towards you, and you'll feel happy making a difference for someone.

The way I see it is that one of the best things about being of service is that it takes you out of your own head. After all, it is impossible to help someone else who is going through a challenging time and at the same time pity yourself. The executive we're calling "Leo" agrees that being of service to others is key to staying far away from executive loneliness. As he stated, "I take on personal commitments to teach others, run workshops, or simply connect with people as a deliberate part of my schedule to ensure I stay in a regular rhythm of contact with others. While previously I would have seen these as a burden on my already busy schedule, I now see them as a pleasurable way to help others and learn at the same time."

Service and My Recovery Journey

When I joined my support group, I was told, "To keep it we have to give it away." I did not fully understand what this meant in the beginning, but they explained to me that commitment and service were part of recovery. I argue that it is part of any and every successful recovery, whether that be recovery from alcohol addiction or from executive loneliness.

We need to make sure that we give back the gifts if we've learned something and found our way. Also, the best way to make sure we don't lose our way is to share all we've learned to help others suffering a similar situation. That's essentially what the support group's guiding statement, "To keep it we have to give it away," means. How this worked in the support group was like this: there were people that helped me to find the program, and I was guided in my own recovery by someone from the group who had gone through it before. That individual personally helped me. The idea is that you give that same gift back to someone else later, which is why the program keeps working and evolving, because there are always new people coming in and the old-timers keep helping the newcomers.

When I first joined the support group, I was very quickly asked to be of service. In the beginning, this could be something as simple as setting up tables, helping out, and sharing stories. When you're one or two months into the process, someone new might come in. If someone who is 10 or 30 years into recovery, approaches the new person and gives them advice, it might be too big for the newcomer to grasp. It ends up demotivating the newcomer, which is where someone like me, only a few years into recovery, can be ready to step in and be of service. I found that being of service gave me a deeper connection with my fellows, and it made me feel good. When I then went out in the world, I carried this strength with me, a day at a time.

I now attend around three to four support group meetings most weeks, including chairing at least one of them. I am there for my own recovery, but also to serve newcomers who are coming for the first time, or to support the fellow that has relapsed and is coming back into the room, to get their feet on the ground again to restart their recovery.

The entire time I was doing the support group program, being of service was always on my mind. Even after "graduating", I am still trying to be of service. That's why I set up the charity campaign; because my colleague and friend died by suicide and I wanted to make a difference. That is something I continue to work hard on to this day. So far, I have donated all of the proceeds from my "Executive Loneliness" keynote addresses to organizations like the Samaritans of Singapore (SOS) to help more people. And I continue to promote this charity and be of service.

I present my keynote address to various groups around the world, where I share my story and experience to lend strength, provide hope, and really help people. So, delivering the keynote itself, and donating any proceeds, are a two-in-one way that I can be of service.

Sign up to volunteer at one of your local charities and join like-minded others who are finding fulfillment, connection, and joy in their greater lives by giving back through serving others.

Have a Plan B

While a common argument is that if you have a plan B, you may not be able to focus on your goals and may not achieve what you want, I dare to differ. I strongly believe that you should not put all your eggs in one basket. I have learnt this the painful way. The job situation is unpredictable these days. The days when you work 20 years in the same company and get a gold watch, are gone. Your company may be loyal to you in the good times, but in the challenging times, they will let you go in a heartbeat. You need to think about your plan B early on. By putting effort into your plan B even while you hold your current executive position, you can decrease any stress and anxiety you might be feeling about job security, which, of course, keeps feelings of executive loneliness at bay.

My Journey With and Without a Plan B

My experience has been that of a typical ex-pat, in the sense that I worked extremely hard for companies and put in long hours, and didn't have much time to build a network outside of my organization. When I was laid off the first time, and the second time when my company was sold, I was taken by complete surprise. It was like somebody ripped the rug out from under me, and I was left completely empty. Naturally, this catapulted me into feelings of isolation, anxiety, and depression.

I didn't have a plan B to fall back on. I didn't even have an updated resume. The last time it happened, I was so paralyzed that I couldn't even think about what to do next. I didn't know where to start. My resume wasn't even in English, and I wasn't in contact with any recruiters, so I was very ill-prepared. And it hit me hard, both in Vietnam and in Indonesia. I panicked, had frequent anxiety attacks, and it brought me to my knees—very serious executive loneliness. I'm blessed just to be alive today, having recovered from my state back then.

Currently, even when everything is going well for me and my career, I've started to question what I should do to make sure this doesn't happen again. If I find myself in the same situation of suddenly losing my job, what should I do? In order to bring me, in the present moment, a sense of control and confidence, and to prepare me to be proactive and not plummet into executive loneliness in the future, I'm making efforts to develop a robust plan B. This is something I've spoken about to many people, which goes back to the section *Step 2—Asking for Help*. I've done everything, including working with a professional writer, so now I have a strong resume. I update my LinkedIn page regularly. I've also formed a habit of asking past employers and people I work with to give me a recommendation on LinkedIn. Rather than a one-and-done project, I see this effort to strengthen my plan B as an ongoing project, to build my profile and update my resume. In turn, should something happen, I have a position of strength that will get me through the door quickly, and should keep dire executive loneliness at bay.

I've learnt that, oftentimes, when you lose your job in a foreign country, you end up stranded because everything in regard to your employment is linked to the job, including your employment pass. When I spoke to my therapist about my anxiety surrounding this hypothetical situation, she told me that you only have 30 days to leave the country after you lose your job in Singapore, due to the visa requirements. That's probably not enough time to find another job.

We talked about how I could feel safer, and she told me there is another employment policy that I could apply for, that would allow me to remain for six months in the country. I did have to pay a bit extra for this safety net, but just by having this, I felt palpably relieved just knowing that I have more time. I also negotiated with my employer for a longer termination clause. I negotiated from a three-month clause to a six-month clause.

This all changed in 2020, though, when COVID-19 became a worldwide issue. I became the franchise owner of a business, but not a business owner myself. This may not have happened if COVID-19 had not disrupted the industry, forcing the head office to try and reduce their risk; and the opportunity came my way. They asked me if I wanted to become a franchise owner. I immediately said no, but my wife convinced me to try it out, because I'd at least have my destiny in my hands. And while I was terrified at first, I'm now feeling good about it, because I know I'm responsible for my own future.

However, I also thought about what might happen if the EGN business went out of fashion, was closed, or I lost the franchise rights. What could I do then? I brainstormed together with a coach, and we looked at my resume and where my strengths lie. I was able to build a career plan. As a result, I studied to become an ICF-certified coach. At the time of writing,

I've completed the training. I just need to do some more hours, and I will be certified. This means I now have a second career as an executive coach. I've been working abroad since 1998, so while consulting is something I could do, coaching has now been added to my resume. While I now coach part-time, I have full-time coaching as a plan B on the back burner. I tell you this to inspire you to put something on your back burner as well. It is empowering and staves off executive loneliness.

I have also built my own website, which you can check it out here: www.nickjonsson.com. My website presents my experience and how people can work with me. This is also a platform where I can incorporate services such as coaching. Thus, it is another potential future career plan, a plan B to fall back on. I'm also saving now to buy myself some property, perhaps in Bali or Lombok, where my wife and I can rent out an apartment, that could be our future retirement home. In these ways, I'm proactively working to create a strong plan B, to help me should I need to fall back on it. At the same time, it provides me with confidence in the present. Without that, if I lost my company, surviving the tremendous stress a third time would prove much more difficult.

Having a professional network can also be very good insurance in times of a global crisis, like now when jobs are scarce. Since I work in the professional networking space, I have seen several senior executives locate new jobs through their professional network, a topic we already looked at in-depth, in the chapter *Professional Networks*.

There's a Chinese proverb that goes, "The best time to plant a tree was 20 years ago. The second best time is now." If you haven't yet begun shoring up your professional network, start today. Doing so will not only give you a major head-start should you suddenly need to find a new job position, but it'll provide you with peace of mind and spirit in the present moment, which helps you to avoid executive loneliness.

Chapter Summary—Finding Your Purpose

The fifth and final step for emerging from executive loneliness and staying out of it lies in finding your purpose. According to Brian Tracy, we all must have a major definite purpose for our life. We must have one goal that, if we accomplish it, can do more to help us improve our life than any other single goal. As Brian Tracy once said, "It doesn't matter where you are coming from. All that matters is where you are going."

This section of the book examines *Step 5—Finding Your Purpose* in the following five facets:

One: Create Goals and Write a Gratitude List

Goals: setting goals is an important step in the recovery from mental illness and in emerging from or avoiding executive loneliness. I cannot imagine a large, successful company or a football team that did not have a strategy or clear goals and targets, so how can we as individuals possibly run our own lives in a successful manner without written goals? It's like driving around in the fog, and if we press on and work harder, it is like turning on the car's high beams in the fog, meaning, our lack of direction and inability to see gets even worse! We must write our goals to get crystal clear about what we want to achieve and to clearly articulate our purpose if we are to make progress in our lives.

Gratitude: the aim of a gratitude list is to help people focus on the good things in their life. Humans have a tendency to take the good stuff for granted, but gratitude journaling can prevent this from happening. By keeping a record of the things that you feel grateful for, it will encourage you to take a positive outlook on life.

Two: Find Your Passion-Hobby

Engaging with your passions and your hobbies can lift you from and keep you out of executive loneliness and make your days, weeks, and years more focused and purposeful. To determine what you are passionate about, you must consider what you genuinely love to do. It must come from you. Having a passion for something not only builds your confidence but also your resilience, which ultimately helps your mental health. It then provides stress relief, improves self-esteem, and, like I said, builds resilience. With the long working hours required by executive work these days, it is essential to have a passion outside the office. It is key to mental health.

Three: Find Your Purpose

Kevin Cottam, global nomad, executive coach, and TEDx speaker, said this about living with purpose: "When you have and act with purpose, it makes your life much easier, because when you are walking into conversations, making choices, and leading yourself and others; it comes from a place much bigger than you. It has more air, it is freer, you can be much more productive, and your performance skyrockets with ease. Having a purpose is like being the 'megaphone': the narrow part is your inner voice and the wide part is your voice bellowing out and acting upon what you are authentically giving to the world. When you have a purpose, loneliness disappears because your life has more reason for being."

Four: Be of Service

Being of service, volunteering your time, work, money, etc., provides many benefits to both your mental and physical health. Volunteering helps counteract the effects of stress, anger, and anxiety. Volunteering combats depression. It makes you happy. It increases your self-confidence. And, as already mentioned, volunteering provides a sense of purpose.

Five: Have a Plan B

The days when you work 20 years in the same company and get a gold watch are gone. Your company may be loyal to you in the good times, but in the challenging times, they will let you go in a heartbeat. You need to think about your plan B early on. This includes networking to build up a professional network across industries. By putting effort into your plan B even while you hold your current executive position, you can decrease any stress and anxiety you might be feeling about job security, which, of course, keeps feelings of executive loneliness at bay.

Executive Loneliness and The 5 Steps: A Summary

In concluding this book on recovering from executive loneliness, let's turn to one executive that we are calling "Tony" and read how he described his experience of executive loneliness:

My executive loneliness first emerged on the day that I landed in Singapore. I had been relocated by my company, and I landed from Europe on a Sunday morning and went straight to my temporary accommodation for the month until my family arrived. A whole slew of small things about the accommodation— cramped, no shared amenities such as a gym or pool, etc.—combined with tiredness meant that I felt I had made the wrong decision. My company had negotiated every last dollar of my relocation package, and I felt that they were scrimping on the accommodation they were providing, and I began to wonder whether this was the "broken windows" theory in action for this company. I didn't have to wait long to find out that it was, unfortunately.

Little did I know that I was entering a period where I would be passed over for promotion despite nine panel members selecting me for the position I was then in; long, drawn-out negotiations with customers as I tried to walk the tightrope between what the head of the business wanted and being reasonable; long drawn-out negotiations on anything related to my remuneration; a toxic culture; and ultimately a period of anxiety and depression. If it wasn't for the friendship of a colleague—we joking(ly) referred to each other as "work wife" and "work husband"—I am not sure that I would have made it through this period. Ultimately, I decided that my mental health was more important, and I resigned.

When I asked "Tony" how he managed to get out of this place of executive loneliness, he told me he did the following, which aligns with the five steps I've recommended in this book. In this way, Tony's explanation of his emergence offers a great review of the 5 steps. Here goes:

Step 1—Taking Stock

- Tony got honest with himself about the dire executive loneliness he was feeling and what he could do about it.

- After working through the five steps, he returned to this step again to take stock and ultimately decided to resign as he realized the importance of his own mental health.

Step 2—Asking for Help

- Tony sought psychiatric help and still does today, to help him come to terms with and emerge from the executive loneliness.

- He was honest with his family and close friends that he was finding life very difficult.

- Tony listened to podcasts where experts and others discussed situations similar to what he was enduring and they gave recommendations for emerging.

Step 3—Getting Healthy

- Tony said he did a lot of walking, and he continues to walk a lot today "to manage [his] anxiety and loneliness."

- Tony made healthy changes in his diet: "I gave up afternoon snacks and desserts during my evening meal. I began to eat dinner at 7 pm, and not 9 pm or 10 pm. This means that I often wake up hungry today, which I take as a good sign."

- To relax or feel upbeat, Tony said he listens to music.

Step 4—Nurturing Healthy Relationships

- Tony relied on his good relationship with a work colleague to lift his spirits and stay more positive during the most difficult times at work.

- He was open and honest with his friends and family during his executive loneliness, which provided him with much-needed support.

Step 5—Finding Your Purpose

- Tony spent time on long-haul flights developing a business plan for his own business, thus cultivating a plan B. By doing this, he gave himself a sense of security and possibility for another future job when working at his very stressful, negative, and unpromising job.

- To ground him in the big-picture purpose of his personal and professional life, Tony developed this practice: "I blocked out strategic thinking and planning timing for 90 minutes every Friday morning, and this is something that I still do today." Again, this is Tony building and nurturing a plan B and actively making sure he's living in alignment across all areas of his life.

- Tony identified what was important to him. What he most wanted. This is what he discovered: "I decided that I wanted to see my children grow up." In this way, Tony identified his values and made sure his purpose aligned and continues to align with those values.

Now that you've read this book, you are in a great position to take the steps, one at a time, to get out of executive loneliness and stay out of it. It doesn't mean it is a quick and immediate emergence. And, obviously, it doesn't mean you must do it alone, as repeatedly you've read that engaging with others is essential to recovering. Please go to my website and contact me with any questions, concerns, or even to discuss the possibility of our working together to help you stay out of executive loneliness. Here is my website one more time: **nickjonsson.com**

While this step-by-step effort to recover from executive loneliness might seem daunting at first, it is the most important endeavor of your life. I wish you great success, and I'm here for you.

If you loved this book, please review it on the platform you purchased it from, and also let your friends know about it. It really helps me out!

Working with Nick

I am active on LinkedIn, where I have more than 27,000 followers at the time of writing, most of whom are senior executives, thought leaders, or business owners.

Please follow me at *https://nickjonsson.com/linkedin* where I post relevant content related to the important topics covered in this book. (You may also send me a friend request until I have reached the limit of 30,000 connections.)

As mentioned in this book, I studied in 2020 to become an International Coaching Federation (ICF) coach and I take on a maximum of two to three clients at any given time. If you are interested in working with me, please send me an email at *nij@egn.com* and mention the subject "Coaching". Please include in the email what you need coaching with.

Il am also collaborating with other coaches who have different focus areas, so I am happy to link you up with the most relevant coach if I cannot work with you myself.

My website is: *nickjonsson.com*.

The Executives' Global Network

It doesn't have to be lonely at the top. If you are a senior executive or business owner based in Singapore, Malaysia or Indonesia and interested in how EGN (Executives' Global Network), a confidential peer group, provides support for its members' work-related challenges, please fill in your contact details at *https://www.egnsingapore.com/membership-form*. My friendly colleagues will be in touch to arrange a free 30-minute consultation via phone or a zoom call. You can also sign up for the EGN Singapore newsletter at the bottom of this page: *egnsingapore.com*.

If you are based in other countries (outside Singapore, Malaysia and Indonesia) search for confidential peer groups near you. EGN is also present in some other countries which you can see here: *https://egn.com.*

Don't be shy. Join a professional network of peers dedicated to "Making Each Other Better".

The Leaders Anonymous Network

Designed as a safe, confidential, non-judgmental place where you can be yourself, learn, interact with other members in a similar leadership position, and move forward on your journey to improved mental health with reduced risk of burnout and isolation. Join the Leaders Anonymous Network and become part of our growing community! *https://leaders-anonymous.com*

Related Media Links

Below is a snapshot of Nick Jonsson's related media exposure/articles:

The Business Times
How to overcome executive loneliness
https://www.businesstimes.com.sg/life-culture/how-to-overcome-executive-loneliness

The Business Times
Successful but Lonely at the Top
https://drive.google.com/open?id=15Qe6dZMk-ylUPcXFxeGchQtVJsnIhbL0&authuser=shuxian@pinpointpr.sg&usp=drive_fs

The Business Times
Successful but Lonely at the Top
https://www.businesstimes.com.sg/lifestyle/feature/successful-but-lonely-at-the-top

Money FM 89.3
Weekends: Successful but Lonely at the Top
https://omny.fm/shows/money-fm-893/weekends-successful-but-lonely-at-the-top

The Peak
The Solitude of Success
https://thepeakmagazine.com.sg/interviews/the-solitude-of-success/

The Business Times
Money FM podcast: Successful but lonely at the top
https://www.businesstimes.com.sg/life-culture/money-fm-podcast-successful-but-lonely-at-the-top

The Straits Times
Money FM podcast: Successful but lonely at the top
https://www.straitstimes.com/business/money-fm-893-podcast-successful-but-lonely-at-the-top

People Matters Global
It's lonely at the top: The workplace isolation people don't talk about
https://www.peoplemattersglobal.com/article/employee-engagement/its-lonely-at-the-top-the-workplace-isolation-people-dont-talk-about-25254

The Business Times
Showing care and concern
https://drive.google.com/open?id=1dIzXdXSkSPcMlnIZt14rrh77PHEuHBTK

The Business Times
Showing care and concern
https://www.businesstimes.com.sg/views-from-the-top/showing-care-and-concern

The Straits Times
Lonely leaders
https://drive.google.com/open?id=1uKJaa8cQdbAoOrsYEz1G6eOcpIk8nR0J

The Straits Times
Lonely leaders
https://www.straitstimes.com/lifestyle/home-design/lonely-leaders

Today's Manager
It's Lonely At The Top In Asia—But It Doesn't Have To Be
https://m360.sim.edu.sg/article/Pages/Its-Lonely-At-The-Top-In-Asia.aspx

INDVSTRVS
Senior Executives Suffering Mental Health Crisis in Isolation
https://indvstrvs.com/senior-executives-suffering-mental-health-crisis-in-isolation/

HR IN ASIA
Lonely at the Top: Leaders in Asia Feel Isolated and Alienated from the Rest of the World
https://www.hrinasia.com/retention/lonely-at-the-top/

HUMAN RESOURCES ONLINE.NEW
It's lonely at the top: How to prevent isolation for your senior executives
https://www.humanresourcesonline.net/its-lonely-at-the-top-how-to-prevent-isolation-for-your-senior-executives/

INDVSTRVS
Executive Loneliness Impacts Performance in Asia
https://indvstrvs.com/executive-loneliness-impacts-performance-in-asia/

People Matters Global
Is digital transformation increasing executive isolation?
https://www.peoplemattersglobal.com/blog/life-at-work/is-digital-transformation-increasing-executive-isolation-23757?

People Matters Global
Could networking be the post-COVID-19 career lifesaver?
https://www.peoplemattersglobal.com/blog/life-at-work/could-networking-be-the-post-covid-19-career-lifesaver-25436

The Peak
Executive isolation and loneliness at the top – and what to do about it
https://thepeakmagazine.com.sg/interviews/executive-isolation-nick-jonsson-egn/

loneliness and depression, but psychologists say it is all right to open up and talk about problems

Chantal Sajan

Two years ago, Mr Nick Jonsson's life hit rock bottom.

He had just reached the summit and landed the job of managing director of EGN Singapore in January 2018.

To all appearances, he seemed to be enjoying the trappings of a successful C-suite executive.

But he struggled with a vague sense of numbness inside and was increasingly isolated from his colleagues as he tried to keep his mental condition a secret for fear of being perceived as a "weak leader".

Away from his parents and young son, who live in Sweden, he turned to alcohol and put on 20kg within three months. His left foot swelled to twice its size and doctors were initially baffled.

Later, it was discovered that the swelling was psychosomatic – triggered by his rapidly deteriorating mental condition.

"I know it is an old cliche, but the saying 'It's lonely at the top' is a great explanation of how it can feel to be the leader of an organisation," says Mr Jonsson, 45, who now lives in Singapore with his second wife, an Indonesian.

"If you are, say, a regional director based in Singapore, you might be reporting to a CEO in the US or Europe. And it's very hard to communicate what is really going on here.

"You probably have a team based all over South-east Asia and you can't talk to them either about your problems because you're supposed to be the 'strong one' who drives the team.

"That means there is no one you can talk to openly about what is ailing you. Taking up the discussion with your family or friends may also not work since they may not understand the unique challenges that you are facing. This can lead to frustration and feelings of isolation."

The problem is likely worse for men as they are not encouraged to show their emotions, he adds.

Mr Jonsson decided to delve deeper into the subject in January last year after an interview with Singapore Press Holdings' radio station Money FM 89.3, in which he was asked to talk about belonging to a network of peers at EGN Singapore.

EGN is a business networking platform for leaders and specialists. It is a branch of a global group set up in 1992, comprising 13,500 members representing more than 8,000 companies.

"It was a sensitive topic and I remember explaining at great length how difficult it is for a senior executive based in Singapore, managing the Asia-Pacific region with its different cultures, markets and legislations," he recalls.

Most of all, he felt like a fraud – although his work was creating business peer networks, he himself could not confide in a single peer in his Singapore office.

A few months later, his close friend, Mr Simon Greaves, a British executive who was based in Singapore, committed suicide at age 50 after hiking to the base camp near Mount Everest.

"Everyone remembered him as an outgoing and fun-loving personality. Nobody would have even suspected that he was suffering in silence," Mr Jonsson remembers.

SMILING DEPRESSION

This is not atypical, according to

At one point in his career, Mr Nick Jonsson found himself lonely, isolated from people and unable to confide in anyone about his stress, and now he wants to share his experience with his book that delves into the world of top executive loneliness. PHOTO: EGN SINGAPORE

LONELY LEADERS

Dr Geraldine Tan, principal psychologist and director of The Therapy Room, who sees many C-suite professionals at her Orchard Road clinic.

Executive loneliness leads to varying degrees of depression which manifests differently, she says.

"There is functioning depression and there is also 'smiling depression'. In functioning depression, a patient is able to carry out his work, but may be quieter and exhibit a constantly low mood level which can last for months.

"In smiling depression, people work hard to hide their pain," she says. "Often, you may mistake them for leading a normal life until they open up to you."

Only within the confines of a doctor's consulting room will such patients reveal their pain and begin to emote, which is the first tentative step towards recovery, says Dr Tan, who has more than two decades of experience treating various psychological problems.

"My patients come to me when it gets too painful to bear. Confiding, crying or just talking about the problem is a huge release for them and that process can even save their lives."

NO ONE TALKS ABOUT IT

After his friend's untimely death, Mr Jonsson embarked on a mission to open up about mental health issues. He started posting on social media, planning for his book and doing surveys of colleagues at his office.

In September last year, he polled all EGN Singapore members on the subject of executive loneliness.

Out of a total of 56 anonymous respondents, 30 per cent said that they had suffered work-related depression.

As to whether they found it easy to talk about the subject, 82 per cent answered "Not easy" and "No".

With the findings, he started to write his first book, Executive Lone-

liness: The Workplace Isolation That People Do Not Talk About, to be released later this year.

He thinks it will be timely as executives additionally grapple with the economic fallout from Covid-19.

American expatriate David Litteken is someone who wrestled with this sense of isolation too.

He is senior vice-president, Asia-Pacific, of BI Worldwide in Singapore, a global agency focused on workforce recognition programmes and sales loyalty events employing more than 1,800 staff worldwide.

Mr Litteken, 53, who has been living here for three years, is responsible for business across the Asia-Pacific, including offices in Shanghai, Singapore, Melbourne and Sydney.

When he was working in Shanghai from 2012 to 2017, he remembers feeling alone in a city of 25 million people.

"I did not know a single person. None of my leaders and none of my staff. I left an environment where I was well-grounded and had to figure it out for myself," he recounts.

He joined a few chambers of commerce and a dining club for executives called Beefsteak & Burgundy and started to build a network of expatriates as well as local Chinese friends.

"That gave me the confidence to reach out further," he recalls.

LONELY AT THE TOP

American Farzana Shubarna, regional director of operations and supply chain for DSM Nutritional Products in Singapore, is another leader who has had to fend off isolation and depression at the top.

Ms Farzana, 46, manages the end-to-end order fulfilment activity for a billion-dollar business.

The Asian-American single mum with two children started her year in operations and supply chain management more than 20 years ago, when the field was male-dominated.

"I worked for years with a sense of not belonging. Any challenges with people or machinery or finance, I had to, by default, manage, deliver and learn on my own," she says. "I knew I had to prove myself to establish credibility, gain respect and have my peers take me seriously.

"I didn't even have any time – or option – to worry about how lonely I was or how strongly I needed to connect and collaborate.

"This loneliness has impacted my personal and family life. I could not speak about my struggles and challenges with anyone at work as I was trying to validate my capability and credibility.

"At home, I was trying not to bring home my work burden. It became a heavy weight on my mind and heart and I accepted it as a growing pain, a rite of passage," she says.

She overcame her feelings of depression and isolation when she left the US three years ago and came to Singapore after being offered the role to lead her company's Asia operations.

"I actively reached out to connect and build a network of friends in Singapore," says Ms Farzana, adding she has also tapped into yoga, meditation and Deepak Chopra to "learn to accept that I do not have to be perfect and my shortcomings make me human".

Psychologist Maria Micha, who works with patients at her Orchard Road clinic to identify the symptoms and root causes of mental disorders, says developing peer networks is healthy for those at the top who are prone to isolation as they work very long stressful hours and do not have time to experience emotional comfort from loved ones.

"Humans are social beings and they have been living in groups since the beginning of time.

"That is how they survived. That is how they evolved and learnt about the world and changed their bodies, their brains and their environment," says the psychotherapist, hypnotherapist and corporate consultant.

The reason one experiences loneliness at the top is that "when you are at the top, you are supposed to have all the answers", says Dr Micha.

"You are supposed to know everything. You cannot expose your vulnerability," she observes.

"You are supposed to be the sovereign, god-like figure that can deal with everything."

But it is especially important for leaders to be transparent that they, too, need help and do not know all the answers.

"That means being vulnerable, but vulnerability does not equal weakness. To be vulnerable means that I allow people to see that I have my own challenges, that I'm being productive about resolving the negative emotions," Dr Micha says.

Five warning signs of executive loneliness

Mental health disorders can be just as dangerous as physical illnesses, but they are not always as easy to detect, says Mr Nick Jonsson, managing director of EGN Singapore.

Depression can affect anyone regardless of age or job seniority, but manifests in different ways.

Watch out for these five danger signs:

1

INTENSE FEELINGS OF ANXIETY AND INSECURITY

Executives may harbour unwarranted suspicions that their employer will fire them at any moment. Or they may turn down new opportunities despite being qualified because they do not feel capable enough.

2

DISTRUST OF COLLEAGUES

Stressed executives may imagine colleagues gossiping about them behind their backs and worry about being back-stabbed.

3

ISOLATION

Sudden withdrawal from social interaction is a definite red flag. Individuals may no longer reach out to friends and family as often as before, which can reinforce feelings of isolation and self-doubt.

4

ADDICTION AND DEPENDENCE ON SUBSTANCES

Corporate leaders may drink or smoke to socialise or relax, but the overuse of such substances to cope with stress may result in poorer health and sleep quality, and lead to a vicious circle of more stress.

5

RECURRING THOUGHTS ABOUT DEATH OR SUICIDE

A sense of impending doom can also compel individuals to give away their prized possessions and make end-of-life plans when they are physically healthy. Immediate psychiatric help is advised when the situation deteriorates at this stage.

* It is advisable to consult a qualified medical professional for any psychological condition that may be of concern.

Helplines

- **National Care Hotline:** 1800-202-6868
- **Institute of Mental Health's Mental Health Helpline:** 6389-2222
- **Singapore Association for Mental Health:** 1800-283-7019
- **Samaritans of Singapore:** 1800-221-4444
- **Silver Ribbon Singapore:** 6385-3714
- **Fei Yue's Online Counselling Service:** www.eC2.sg

AS SEEN IN

Successful But Lonely at the Top, **The Business Times**©

FEATURE

28 FEBRUARY · 01 MARCH

SUCCESSFUL BUT LONELY AT THE TOP

Senior executives under immense pressure to excel have few avenues
to vent their fears and frustrations

HELMI YUSOF

AS COMPANIES WORK through the Covid-19 outbreak, one man worries about the mental health impact it might have on the C-suite executives steering them. He knows the financial stress a crisis like this puts on businesses. When Lehman Brothers collapsed in 2008, his F&B company lost 50 percent of its revenue for nine months, forcing him to eventually sell his entire business to a competitor.

It's heartbreaking, to say the least, to spend 14 years building something, only to lose it all. At the height of its success, the company earned a World Gourmet Summit award, and the man (speaking on conditions of anonymity) received a nomination for Ernst & Young Entrepreneur of the Year. He sat on the boards of various entrepreneur-based organisations and people constantly sought his advice on expansion into China.

But by 2009, his dream life started to unravel. A month after he lost his company, his wife filed for divorce. He fell ill and stayed home alone to recuperate. Left to his own devices with just a few friends to confide in, he sank into depression and entertained suicidal thoughts.

"I had gotten so used to being chauffeured around," he recalls, "and wearing bespoke clothes. Everyone was nice to me because they wanted to get great service when they went to my restaurants. I was shaking hands with ministers. Aspiring entrepreneurs knew my name."

"But when I lost my company, people started avoiding me. The phone stopped ringing, and the only people knocking on my door were debt collectors. To be fair, I don't think people shunned me because they were mean or opportunistic. They just didn't know what to say to me, because they had no idea what it's like to lose a business."

Failure is such a taboo topic in

1

Weekend

AS SEEN IN

Successful But Lonely at the Top, **The Business Times**©

2020   **FEATURE**   9

Singapore that "we as a society collectively fail to address it when it happens," he says. "In recent years, the Singapore government has started to talk about how we should see failure as part and parcel of entrepreneurship, and remove the stigma attached to it. But back in 2009, there was no such recognition... I struggled for years to get back on my feet."

LEADERS HIDE STRUGGLES

While stress is an inevitable component of work life, the pressure can be particularly acute for men and women at the top, says Maria Micha, a clinical mental health counselor and corporate trainer with over two decades of practice.

"I would say that 100 per cent of C-level managers suffer from anxiety. And 70 to 80 per cent of them have mild, moderate or severe depression. About 10 per cent have suicidal thoughts – though only a small percentage of that actually act on it," she says.

"The biggest problem is the taboo surrounding these issues. C-suite execs risk losing their position if they admit they're experiencing depression or contemplating suicide, because there's so much riding on the public perception that their companies are doing well... As a result, many of them don't look for help because they're afraid about word getting out."

Nick Jonsson, managing director of EGN Singapore, kept his condition a secret at first. When he fell into depression in 2018, he started drinking heavily and gaining a lot of weight. At the lowest point of his struggle, he took a trip to Batam for a full health screening – afraid that if he went to a Singapore clinic, someone might recognise him and tattle.

The doctors there gave him a very poor assessment of his health, which consequently spurred him to seek professional help from other doctors, a mental health counselor and a fitness coach. For further treatment, he flew to a Bangkok hospital – again fearful of being spotted in a Singapore clinic.

"Most senior executives won't admit it," he says, "but it's incredibly isolating to be an expatriate in a foreign country. If you are, say, a regional director based in Singapore, you might be reporting to a CEO in the US or Europe. And it's very hard to communicate to them about what's really going on here. You probably have a

(1) Senior execs hide their loneliness, anxiety and depression for fear of losing their hard-earned positions. (2) It's important for people around a depressed person to reach out to him or her, as that person is sometimes in denial. (3) Mental health issues affect all staff levels. (4) It's important to have a few hours a day to unwind on your own. (5) A very depressed person may not reach out for help. (6) Nick Jonsson, MD of EGN Singapore, suffered from depression in 2018.

team based all over South-east Asia and you can't talk to them either about your problems, because you're supposed to be the strong one who drives the team."

"It may be worse for you if you're a man because men aren't encouraged to speak openly. Women find it easier to share their problems with close friends, but men tend to suffer in silence. They have invested so much in the job and made huge sacrifices to be successful, and the last thing they want is to booted out of the job on the grounds that they're mentally unfit."

DATA IS SCARCE

Experts say there is scarce data on how many senior executives suffer from loneliness, depression or anxiety. A 2016 general study by the Institute of Mental

Health published in 2018 showed that one in seven people in Singapore experience a mental health condition in their lifetime.

But when EGN Singapore, a business networking platform for leaders and specialists, conducted a small-sample survey among its members here, it found that 30 per cent of senior executives have undergone bouts of depression – higher than the national average cited above – while over 80 per cent of them are reluctant to discuss the state of their mental health with their companies.

When Mr Jonsson's friend Simon Greaves, the director of a Singapore executive search firm, took his own life in 2019, his brother told Mr Jonsson that Mr Greaves had been facing depression. "And yet all of his friends remembered him as being fun, outgoing and competent at his job," says Mr Jonsson. It was Mr Greaves' death that pushed Mr Jonsson to go public with his own mental health issues, posting personal revelations of his struggles on his LinkedIn profile.

Weekend

AS SEEN IN

Successful But Lonely at the Top, **The Business Times**©

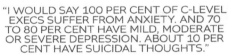

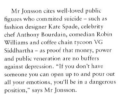

"I WOULD SAY 100 PER CENT OF C-LEVEL EXECS SUFFER FROM ANXIETY. AND 70 TO 80 PER CENT HAVE MILD, MODERATE OR SEVERE DEPRESSION. ABOUT 10 PER CENT HAVE SUICIDAL THOUGHTS."

–
MARIA MICHA

Mr Jonsson cites well-loved public figures who commited suicide – such as fashion designer Kate Spade, celebrity chef Anthony Bourdain, comedian Robin Williams and coffee chain tycoon VG Siddhartha – as proof that money, power and public veneration are no buffers against depression. "If you don't have someone you can open up to and pour out all your emotions, you'll be in a dangerous position," says Mr Jonsson.

Ms Micha notes: "Singapore only decriminalised suicide in May 2019 – which was the right thing to do. For years, I would get calls from potential clients who ask: 'If I tell you I have suicidal thoughts, would you report me?' Even when I answer, 'No, never', they were still afraid… If Singapore wants to maintain its position as a business hub, it must also lead the way in corporate mental health."

MENTAL HEALTH FOR ALL

Although Ms Micha, Mr Jonsson and EGN are mostly looking at mental issues among men and women at the top, other health experts insist the issue affects all levels of a corporation.

Priyanka Bajpai, regional head, Southeast Asia, of healthcare communications firm SPAG, says: "Mental health is not bound by hierarchy, and anyone is susceptible to issues such as loneliness, anxiety and depression. The pressure to create a brand for oneself and one's company, to engage in social media and stay publicly visible, to fulfill KPIs and other measures of success, all bear upon the individual.

"Hence, it's not so much a function of leadership, but the expectation of the individual from themselves, as well as how they manage and perform, while still maintaining sanity in pressure situations. In fact, one could argue that millennials face a greater pressure to project a certain image of corporate success on social media, whereas older executives are more secure of their track record and have their coping strategies in place.

"The pressures we face are inevitably part and parcel of our contemporary

(1 - 3) Mental health issues remain a taboo in Asian cultures, though there are signs things may be changing. (4) Priyanka Bajpai of healthcare communications firm SPAG. (5) Maria Micha, a clinical mental health counsellor and corporate trainer.

lifestyles today, but the degree to which we prioritize our mental health is the degree to which we can improve and work upon it."

Both Ms Bajpai and Ms Micha note that more organisations are recognising the importance of mental health and reaching out to experts. The National Council of Social Service has a Mental Health Toolkit For Employers that provides resources for employers to support employee mental health. Many companies are teaching employees to reach out to a colleague empathetically when they spot warning signs, such as alcoholism, excessive weight gain and despondency.

But mental health programmes looking specifically at C-suite struggles are less common, because senior execs prefer to conceal them from staff and shareholders. As Ms Micha put it: "Companies really need to look deeper at the issue if they want to improve their KPIs and increase their sales. Any financial investment in staff counselling will pay back in spades. When an executive is free from the hormones of stress, that's when they can be creative and innovate, seek solutions that were not visible before, and take the company to a higher level. Companies must remove the stigma of anxiety, depression and mental illness, so employees feel safe speaking about their problems."

08-11 Cover Story.indd   10-11

AS SEEN IN

Successful But Lonely at the Top, **The Business Times**©

CONFESSIONS OF A LOCAL EX-CEO

I'm Singaporean and for 14 years I built an F&B company that expanded from Singapore into China. I've been lauded as a model entrepreneur and featured in newspapers and magazines many times. I had operations in Singapore, Shanghai and Beijing. When Lehman Brothers collapsed in 2008, triggering the Great Financial Crisis, my company lost 50 percent of our sales (which per month averaged S$450,000) for nine months.

Out of desperation, we sold the company, lock, stock and barrel, to a competitor. I had hoped they'd keep me, but they didn't. Soon after that, I went into a spiral.

My wife divorced me within a month, though fortunately we didn't have kids and she didn't ask for maintenance. I fell sick and had to stay out of the public eye for months. The phone stopped ringing, and the only people knocking on my door were debt collectors.

When your business fails, people don't remember the 10 good things you did before that – like supporting young entrepreneurs or helping the country's F&B industry develop – they just remember that your business failed. You go into a tailspin, and suicidal thoughts emerge. I fantasised many times about jumping off my building, because I was so depressed. But luckily there were moments of grace that saved me.

I remember a friend who came by and we didn't talk the whole night – we just watched soccer. I don't even like soccer, but I stared at the TV screen for 45 minutes, because I was just happy to be sitting next to my friend, who cared enough to just spend time with me. There's no judgment – that was important.

Another time, a friend asked me out for a birthday lunch. When I arrived there were a dozen of my friends there. They didn't get me a present, but they all each put in S$100 in an envelope and gave me S$1,500 or so. It's not the money, of course, that mattered. It's the gesture that moved me.

Eventually I met a single mother with two kids. Kids, if you don't already know, are great. They don't judge you at all. I played with them when I was there. And I slowly realised there were so many things in life besides career success. And I began to pick myself up and rebuild my life. I'm in my early 50s now and starting a new business. It'll take me some years to grow this one. But, as they say, baby steps.

When you're down and out, you're too depressed to save yourself. The only thing that can save you is human connection. I hope people reading remember that when someone is depressed, it's up to them to reach out and show compassion to the person. They don't have to say anything smart or insightful. Just visit the person and be present – that's enough. That might save that person's life.

> "A friend asked me out for a birthday lunch. When I arrived there were a dozen of my friends there. They didn't get me a present, but they all each put in S$100 in an envelope and gave me S$1,500 or so. It's not the money, of course, that mattered. It's the gesture that moved me."

CONFESSIONS OF AN EXPAT EX-BDM

> "Fortunately I have a good wife who was observing everything that was going on. It was she who pulled me out of it – as things were going south very quickly."

I'm from Germany and I worked as the Business Development Manager for an oil-and-gas service company in Singapore from 2014 to 2017. It was a fairly new company and I had poured all my savings into it. We thought we would sell it later for a lot of money, which would then be our nest egg. I brought my wife and three children to Singapore, having sold everything we had in Germany.

When the O&G market collapsed in 2015, the interested party who wanted to buy our company backed out, our Chinese partner backed out, and we were facing US$3 million in debt, with no revenue coming in. We could not fix the problems because it was an industry-wide downturn. It was mayhem.

For much of 2016, I was still going into the office, but I didn't have anything to do. I was anxious and distracted all the time. Even when there were potential opportunities or silver linings, the fear of failure overwhelmed me. I kept thinking I had failed my wife and children. My boss had properties and some inheritance money, so he couldn't really understand what I was going through. We would hang out after work and drink. But that became a spiral that got progressively darker.

Fortunately I have a good wife who was observing everything that was going on. It was she who pulled me out of it – as things were going south very quickly. When I felt guilty about bringing the family here, she said this was their choice as much as it was mine. She never made me feel bad about myself.

When the company was bought over by a rival, I made many attempts at get another job elsewhere, but they came to naught. I have only an Employment Pass, and companies didn't want the hassle of the handling my paperwork. Again my wife came to the rescue, helping me make the decision to start my own events consultancy firm here. Even though she had not worked a day since we got married, she started working everyday with this startup.

Meanwhile, the friends I thought I had had stopped talking to me. They were friendly as long as I had a job and money. But the moment I lost those things, they ceased to care. I imagine that if I was a single expatriate man going through this alone, I might have done something drastic to myself.

My advice to any single expat is to just pack up and go home to the people you love, because they're the only ones who can help you through this. If you don't, you may end up looking for sympathy or escape in all the wrong places, and it'll only get you into more trouble. Without the right support system when things go south, you will be in for a very rough ride.

Support Contacts and Hotlines

Below are my contact details as well as a list of the coaches and mentors who helped me with my recovery and self-development journey. I am still working with many of them today as I want to continue to forever learn and improve myself to become a better human being, father, husband, and co-worker.

While most of them are located in Singapore, where I am based, you can also work with them remotely online.

Please note this list was accurate at the time of writing but may change over time. If you have any issues, visit our online resources page via our Book Bonus website: *https://executivelonelinessbook.com/page/bonus*

Nick Jonsson

Co-Founder & Managing Director with EGN (Executives' Global Network) Singapore

https://nickjonsson.com/linkedin

nij@egn.com

EGN Singapore

https://www.egnsingapore.com/

Fill in this form if interested in becoming a member: https://sg.egn.com/become-a-member-of-egn

Sign up for the EGN Singapore newsletter at the bottom of this page: https://www.egnsingapore.com/

info.sg@egn.com

Maria Micha Counselling Center

Counseling, psychotherapy, hypnotherapy, corporate training and health coaching

Sentosa, Singapore

+ 65 8189 6386

mariamicha.com.sg

Dr. Glenn Graves

Psychologist & Professional Life Coach

Call/Whatsapp: +65 9636-8060

http://www.counselingperspective.com/glenn-graves

http://www.coachingperspective.com

http://www.Mindfulpathway.com

Alexander Mearns

Health practitioner, founder of Levitise—Holistic Lifestyle Centre

https://www.levitise.com.sg/

Andy Lopata

Author, Professional Speaker& Professional Relationships Strategist

https://lopata.co.uk/

Avni Martin

ICF professional certified coach

https://martinccs.com/coach-training/

Alice Wikström

Mindfulness Coach

https://www.alicewikstrom.com/

Andrew Bryant

Executive Coach

https://www.selfleadership.com/

Ritu G. Mehrish

Executive Coach and Author of Leader's Block

ritu@ritumehrish.com

https://www.ritumehrish.com/

Avi Liran

"Chief Delighting Officer"

He is an expert consultant, TEDx speaker and mentor, who helps people to create delightful leadership and positive culture transformation.

https://www.aviliran.com/

Kevin Cottam

Executive Leadership Coach and Professional Keynote Speaker

https://www.thenomadicmindset.com/

Grant "Axe" Rawlinson

Decision-Making Coach and Human Powered Explorer

https://www.powerful-humans.com/about-powerfulhumans

Todd Gilmore

Fitness Coach

WA: +971503979615

todd@theenduranceacademy.com

Marcus and Sari Marsden

Authors of *Fit to Lead*

https://fittoleadbook.com/

Jeff Goh

Owner of JeffGoh Total Fitness

Strength and conditioning. Nutrition. Clinical Sports Massage.

https://www.instagram.com/jeffgohtotalfitness/?hl=en

Phillip Kelly

Body Expert Coach

http://bodyexpertsystems.com/

Chris Richards

Managing Director APAC and Middle East at Ultimate

https://www.linkedin.com/in/chrisrichardspt/

https://ultimateperformance.com

Simon McKenzie (Mac)

Managing Director, Asia Pacific at Bridge

www.bridge-partnership.com

Andrew da Roza

Psychotherapist - Addictions

PROMISES HEALTHCARE

Singapore

(+65) 6397 7309

www.promises.com.sg

Singapore Helplines

For my Singapore friends here is a list of Singapore helplines. You may search in google for this kind of association in your respective country.

Samaritans of Singapore: 1800-221-4444

Singapore Association for Mental Health: 1800-283-7019

Care Corner Counselling Centre (Mandarin): 1800-353-5800

Institute of Mental Health's Mental Health Helpline: 6389-2222

Alcoholics Anonymous (AA) Hotline: +65 8112 8089

Silver Ribbon: 6386-1928

Shan You Counselling Centre (Mandarin): 6741-0078

Fei Yue's Online Counselling Service: www.eC2.sg

Tinkle Friend (for primary school children): 1800-2744-788

Executive Loneliness Resource Kit

It doesn't have to be lonely at the top. Join our community and get access to our ever-growing tips and resources. In addition, you can access the links mentioned in this book.

Your journey is yet to begin until you start to implement the ideas in this book. After all, implementation and action-taking are the real keys to success.

Visit
https://executivelonelinessbook.com/page/bonus
to join our community and get access
Executive Loneliness Resource Kit

Scan the QR Code Below